Moving Mama

Taking Care of Mother During Her Final Years With Alzheimer's

By Anne Hays Egan

Edited by Pat D'Andrea

Moving Mama

DEDICATION

This book is dedicated to Mama; my aunts, Tula and Sister; and my grandmother, Gram. They were all wonderful, strong Southern women who each were trailblazers in their own right. They left a wonderful legacy to those of us who now carry their stories.

Hattie Hays Whorton, "Gram" – 1882-1982
Helen Margaret Whorton White, "Sister" – 1904 -1995
Mary Carolyn Whorton Kinser, "Tula" – 1911 -2000
Lorene Anne Whorton Egan, "Mama" – 1917 -2002

ACKNOWLEDGMENTS

I would like to thank my family, my brother Tom and sister-in-law Ann who cared for mother in Louisville; and especially my brother John, who is an amazing human being and who provided mother with such exceptional care at the end of her life. Thanks also to mama's caregivers and friends, who were so helpful: Mary and Baird, Louise and her friends from Parkway Presbyterian in Winston. Robin in Louisville. And, in Buffalo, WY: Corinne, Jolene, Dottie, Mary Pat and her staff and friends at United Church of Buffalo, WY. Thanks to my Aunt, Tula (deceased) who talked with us and with mama so often; who provided calm counsel and support; and who was always there for her little sister.

To my cousins who read the book and provided such helpful feedback and suggestions, thank you Jenny, Carolyn and Margaret.

A special thanks go to my friends who read the manuscript and provided wonderful suggestions and quotes: Betty, Catherine, Claire, Debbie, Jane A., Jerri, Marian, Michael M., Michael S., Nancy, Ron, and Vivian. And, thanks to my editor, Pat D'Andrea.

Table of Contents

Introduction 1

Chapter 1: Difficult Discoveries 11

Chapter 2: Trying to Make Sense of Things 19

Chapter 3: The Will and The Government 27

Chapter 4: Protecting Her Finances 35

Chapter 5: Standing Up To Others 43

Chapter 6: Summer Visit to Santa Fe and Travel Challenges 53

Chapter 7: Hiring, Firing and Blowing Smoke 63

Chapter 8: Considering Options for Her Care 73

Chapter 9: Striking Out and Striking a Bargain 81

Chapter 10: Taking Care of Ourselves - Mindfulness and Self Care 93

Chapter 11: Packing and the Farewell Party 99

Chapter 12: Driving Down to Georgia 103

Chapter 13: Difficult Family Relationships 107

Chapter 14: Adjusting to Louisville & Selling the Winston House 119

Chapter 15: When They Forget Who You Are 121

Chapter 16: Tough Choices and Taking Charge 127

Chapter 17: Stories and Playacting 133

Chapter 18: Getting Help Around the House 137

Chapter 19: Finding Entertainment: The Magic of Music 141

Chapter 20: Friskies and Milk for Breakfast 147

Chapter 21: Health Problems, Hospital and Rehab 153

Chapter 22: TSA Mishaps Mess Up Travel 159

Chapter 23: Afternoon Drives in the Bighorns 165

Chapter 24: Nutritional Challenges: Getting Her to Eat 169

Chapter 25: Personal Care, Dr. Whorton's RX and Skin Treatments......173

Chapter 26: Managing Sundowners – Summer at Columbia...................177

Chapter 27: Taking Time and Living in the Now....................................181

Chapter 28: Thanksgiving, My Last Visit with Mama 185

Chapter 29: Her Last Day - Debussy, Good-byes and the 23rd Psalm...187

Resources for Caregiving...193

About The Author 200

Introduction

This provides an introduction to my Mother, Lorene Anne Whorton Egan. She was born September 28th, 1917 and died December 17th, 2002. She was the youngest of four children born to Hattie Hays Whorton (1882-1982) and Dr. William Walker Whorton (1877-1950).

Dr. Whorton was a physician who graduated from Vanderbilt Medical School when he was 23 years old, in the late 1890s. He helped start one of the large nonprofit hospitals in Birmingham soon after the turn of the century. When Mother was five years old, her appendix burst, and he rushed her to the hospital, performing life-saving surgery that was seldom successful back in 1922. Because he died before I was born, I didn't know him except through stories told by different family members, all with varying perspectives based on their own experiences with him. One of my cousins talked about how she would visit him at his clinic after school, and he would talk philosophy, religion and politics with her in between seeing patients; and that he was one of the few physicians at that time who saw both white and black patients. Another family member mentioned that he began to drink more over time, and that things became more difficult. At any rate, Grandmother separated from him, but never divorced. And she cared for him during his final months when he was ill and hospitalized.

Mother's Mama Hattie was an artist and musician. She was as low-keyed as her husband was high strung. Gram (as we called her) was a very loving and a somewhat distracted Mother to her children. She had gone to private school and college at Athens in north Alabama in the late 1800s and early 1900s when few women were afforded those opportunities. Hattie painted portraits of

Stonewall Jackson, Jefferson Davis and Alabama House Speaker Bankhead, which hang in the Montgomery Museum to this day. The Bankhead family member best known to most people is the Speaker's daughter, Tallulah, who left Alabama for New York at an early age and never looked back. Gram was one of those few well known women artists in the Deep South in the early decades of the 20th century who was actually able to make a living with her art work. Family members still treasure her paintings, art deco painted china, and her Joan of Arc gold-leaf plate that won the Alabama Fair Blue Ribbon in 1927.

Although this has never been medically tested or proven, many of our family members believe that somewhere a number of generations back, some of our ancestors had "bad blood," as we say in the South. We could trace many of Mother's ancestors back – way, way back. One of our earliest ancestors, Sir Thomas was titled by King Henry VIII in 1544; his Great Grandson, Philip Lord Whorton was a puritan, immortalized by Van Dyck and his foundation that still gives away Bibles. However, his grandson (another Philip) made trouble in two countries, and died in disgrace (and reportedly of syphilis) in a monastery in Spain.

Great Grandfather Asa B. Hays had a similar long history, though as a Scot going back to the 1300s. Who knows, some of Hay Clan and the Whortons could have come to blows over King James. We always thought it was interesting that our Great Grandfather Hays had been a judge in North Alabama during Reconstruction. Turns out that he may have been something of a rake. His socializing activities when he was a Confederate while stopped in Tennessee may or may not have had something to do with his decision to switch at that point to the Union Side, and leave town. Our big family "secret" was that Asa B. Hays served in the Union Army. We were so excited to discover this secret when we were going

2

through old trunks after Mama died. My brother, a historian, found a Union Army Cap with a Captain's insignia, buttons, and GAR encampment ribbons! So, that was why he was given a judgeship!

We can say, like most families, we had a lot of good history we often claim, as well as some rather bad behavior along the way, which we'd just as soon not.

Mother was a beautiful and brilliant child. She was an exceptionally smart and diligent student. Double-promoted in her early years, she graduated from high school at age 15, and entered the University of Alabama just before her 16th birthday, during the Great Depression. After graduating from college, she began a career teaching English at a high school in Birmingham, Alabama. Like most young single women of the time, she lived at home with her Mother.

Mama was recruited by the American Red Cross to serve as a Club Director during World War II, which was one of the high points of her life. She and the group of young women recruited along with her travelled to the west coast by train, and then went to Hawaii and Guam together (by plane). They spent weeks in training and formed close bonds. Many remained friends for most of the rest of their lives. Mother served in Guam and Tinian. She was there when the crew of the Enola Gay took off on their bombing run over Hiroshima, and was there when they returned. Like so many of what Brokaw called "The Great Generation," she said little about the difficult times, but was a stalwart. In fact, all she ever said to us about that night they bombed Hiroshima was they looked like they were in shock when they came back from Japan.

Once or twice, she talked about how she and her staff would go onto the naval ships when they returned from battle and help the sailors write letters home. She did not often speak about how many last letters they helped the young men write, or the impact on her soul of the hours spent with the dying and the dead. In a letter she wrote to her Mother sometime after the war, she mentioned that as glad as she was to see the war ended, she could not imagine how difficult it must have been for families in Japan. Like Scarlett in *Gone with the Wind*, she simply did what was needed. And, like her, she preferred to tell the more positive stories - like how, at the end of the war, at a celebration dinner, she met an officer who had just received a surrender sword from one of the islands. He gave the sword to her for her safekeeping that evening.

Mother had many stories of and pictures about her time in Red Cross during World War II. Some of my favorites are one of all of the Red Cross staff in Guam, and one of her on the Oahu overlook after the war (both are in the book's picture gallery). Another favorite is one of Honolulu in the 1940s, with the big old hotel (now the Sheraton) on the right, Diamond Head on the left, and nothing in between but beautiful beach (whereas today it is jammed with high rises)! There were lots of pictures of the club, people singing, and very few images that showed the dangers and horrors of war.

After the war, Mama returned to Alabama and was in charge of the Hospital Red Cross in Montgomery where she met my Father, a Red Cross Assistant Field Director. Dad was given the task of teaching her how to drive. It must have been a very special Driver's Ed experience for them, because they dated and married.

After the war, many women were surprised to discover that much of their newfound freedom and occupational status quickly dissipated as the men returned to take back their jobs. In the Deep South, women of a certain class were not expected to work after marriage. The Red Cross asked Mother to stay on as the Hospital Field Director after she married Dad, which was a tribute to her value to them. However, once she was pregnant with me, she did the appropriate thing and resigned to become a Mother.

She was a fulltime Mother during the early and mid-1950s while they lived in Alabama, and she had Mary, who took care of me, and later my brother Tom. Then, in 1955, Dad received an assignment from the Red Cross to move to post-war France. He left before we did, and then Mother moved us to Ft. Hamilton, NY to await a ship to take us to France. I'm not sure how long we stayed in those temporary quarters awaiting orders and a transport ship, but I can remember being there, and it must have been a real hassle for Mother.

My Father had found us a beautiful but war damaged chateau in Chamblais, France. Pictures of us in front of the chateau show a beautiful multi-acre front lawn with a circular drive. What you can't see in the picture are the holes in the roof caused by bombing during the war. From the inside, you could see the sky through the holes. Tom and I were forbidden to go up there, and, of course, we had to check it out.

The pipes in the house froze during the cold winter of 1956, while we were moving to Mctz. Gram came to spend a good bit of time with us in Europe, once with her best friend, Aunt Blanche, and once by herself. Gram took me to Paris with her many times on the train, and she had permission to copy some of the artwork in the Louvre. Paris remains one of my favorite cities to this day.

Mother drove me to school, which was a little one-room schoolhouse in Chamblais. She made a home for us, and managed our many trips throughout Europe. She made sure that we learned about the history, art and music of the many countries where we lived and visited. I can remember standing in the large plaza in front of the Vatican, tired and thirsty; and standing in the late afternoon sunlight in Notre Dame, transfixed by the rose window. We spent one Christmas in Garmisch, and I can still remember terrifying trips in winter through the Alps. My youngest brother, John, was born in the little military hospital in Chamblais and has dual citizenship (U.S. and France). He should make his native country proud, as he speaks the best French of all of us, and served as our French-speaking tour guide when all of us returned to Europe together many years later.

After our time in Europe, we settled in St. Petersburg, Florida. Mother managed the house and the children, and I can remember her walking us to the beach many times, taking a short cut through the neighbor's yard. I remember visiting Dad's Red Cross office in the old Don Caesar hotel. It was quite interesting to discover on one of my consulting projects decades later that the hotel had been saved and renovated. It remains an area landmark, a gorgeous large pink art deco building. My Father's office would have been somewhere in what is now air over the lobby entrance.

Following St. Petersburg, we moved to Pinehurst, North Carolina and then to Montgomery, Alabama. Mother must have been thrilled to be back "home," and a short distance from her Mother. From this point on, wherever we lived, Mother and we children spent all summer each summer in Birmingham. Now that her children were all in school, Mother went back to work in the early 1960s. She taught music and worked for the Girl Scouts. It was an extremely volatile time both in Montgomery and in our household. There were frequent arguments. Dad was drinking, and Mother was finding her voice.

Alabama was a very difficult place to live in the late 1950s and early 1960s. Montgomery celebrated its Civil War Centennial for most of 1961, and almost everyone I knew (white folks) dressed up in antebellum garb once a week to celebrate. Celebrate? The bus boycotts had just happened, and the Freedom Riders were coming soon. You could cut the fear with a knife. White violence was frightening and incomprehensible to me.

I remember my shock and dismay when the ***Birmingham News*** reported on the four girls who were bombed in the 16th Street Baptist Church in Birmingham in 1963. We were all there in Birmingham visiting Gram that summer. Adults whispered in attempts to keep their own fears away from their children. At 13, I felt I wasn't really a child anymore and wanted to know what the adults were saying. I remember overhearing Mama express sadness and concern over the senseless violence. That day, I spent a good deal of time by myself in Gram's back yard, just sitting and thinking. It was at that point that I began to realize that there was something fundamentally broken with the culture I had been taught to revere from the cradle on.

We moved to San Juan, Puerto Rico that fateful summer of 1963. Dad had been working quietly to get transferred out of Montgomery and its toxic influence. The move to San Juan was liberating for us children. Perhaps for Dad as well. I think it was probably more devastating for Mother than we realized. Dad's drinking increased, and Mother threatened to leave him, take the kids and move back to Birmingham with her Mother. She demanded that he go see Chaplain Diaz, who was the minister at the Protestant Chapel. He agreed to all of her demands, stopped drinking cold turkey, and focused on work and family. As time progressed, when he wasn't consumed with Red Cross disaster emergencies (like the Haitian Crisis where hundreds of people were airlifted from Haiti to Puerto Rico), he spent most evenings in the library or the woodworking shop until either closed for the day and he returned home.

Soon after she found her voice, Mother began to lose her moorings and have screaming fits. She would come completely unglued, running around the house, throwing things, and often hitting us. In public, we and our neighbors pretended not to notice. I babysat for most of the neighbors and was out of the house as much as possible. My middle brother mowed lawns and played golf. My youngest brother, John, was home and got the brunt of her craziness. That's what we called it. There were few mental health resources, and nobody who was anybody would be caught dead using them back then. One year, Mother taught school fulltime, and the other three years she taught music and was a substitute school teacher.

In spite of all of the discord and difficulty at home, we three children loved Puerto Rico. Living in a multi-racial culture was a new and delightful experience that shaped us forever. We loved going to a school with lots of other smart kids, and learning from teachers who loaded us up with challenges and homework. I attended Teen Bandstand at Ft. Brooke, and watched with amusement as my friend Bob Bird outfoxed the tourists who asked the 6"2" blond teen if he had seen Americans much, and he told them the long tale of his life as a poor Puerto Rican child, ending with 'Yeah, I lived in Chicago for ten years. It's OK.'

We traveled around the Caribbean. Mother signed John up for piano lessons and me up for violin lessons at the Conservatory of Music, and we attended the Casals Festivals each summer. Here, as in Europe and Montgomery, Mother was our family's director of culture and tourism. She was also an active volunteer in the church and community.

We moved back to the U.S. and Louisville, Kentucky in 1967 for my senior year in high school, not a propitious time. Mother began teaching piano in earnest during those years, and spent most of the rest of her life as a piano teacher with many students and a full schedule. After the first year in Louisville, I went away to college. So my relationship with her began to shift. Although I was not yet an adult in her eyes, and often didn't act like one, I was more than ready to try to strike out on my own. I was away for college and graduate school, and spent many of the summers at Brevard Music Camp. While I was in college, my Father received his final transfer to run the Red Cross VA office in Winston-Salem, North Carolina.

They moved to a lovely place in what would be their last and long-term permanent home. For over thirty years, they lived in and loved Winston. By this time, they had built a nice asset base. Decades of deprivation and saving that had been drilled into them by early experiences in the Depression had now provided them with a very comfortable life. Their assets allowed them luxuries they had denied themselves in previous years. They enjoyed trips to the Outer Banks, and the Northeast (Dad's home area). They went to Europe and the British Isles.

My Father became sick with lymphoma in the late 1970s. He managed a successful remission for six or seven years, then cancer recurred with flare-ups confusing is it just "the cancer recurred?" about every two years until 1992 when he died. He had the dubious honor of being Bowman Gray's longest living lymphoma patient when he died, exhausted from battles He had been tiny and jaundiced, and he asked that we take good care of Mother. We

9

think we did. Dad had taken good care of us, and left significant assets. The brokerage accounts were in Mother's name with transfer on death arrangements to the three of us, which protected the assets from excessive taxation and gave Mother all she needed for the rest of her life, and more.

When my Father died Mother discovered that she was exhausted from years of caregiving. She was thin and became sick with an ear infection soon after his death. In the years following, she continued teaching, and still had a large piano class. She was the President of Presbyterian Women at the church for some years, and active in the local Music Teachers' Association, serving as its President for a while as well. The few years after Dad's death were very full, and she was quite happy. What we didn't realize was that after my Father died she began to show some very early problems with her memory.

By the mid 1990s, we could see that she was slipping.

Chapter 1: Difficult Discoveries

Perhaps the changes weren't that subtle. But then we weren't expecting them. After all, Mother was very smart – double promoted and sent to college at the tender age of not-quite-16. In addition to being exceptionally smart, Mama was well-organized, and always in charge. So the possibility of her having Alzheimer's didn't really hit us until it was obvious.

I think that's the case for many of us.

But there we were in the mid 1990s,facing a conundrum. My brother was examining her bank statement when a $12,000 expense caught his eye. It was rather hard to miss, since the mortgage was paid off, and Mother had few expenses. Gradually, we pulled the story out of her. She explained that some very nice men had come by her house one day and told her they were roofers. They explained they had noticed some problems with her roof that needed to be addressed quickly before other problems developed and winter came.

We had to pull that story out of her a little bit at a time over many days and weeks. She was unwilling to talk much about it, and was defensive. So, at some level, she must have had some concerns about the huge expenditure that she made so quickly.

Finally, in bits and pieces, we got the gist of the situation. Being full of Southern hospitality, Mother chatted with them, and allowed them to show her the areas where the roof was damaged. It seems as if, after not much more than a little conversation, Mother agreed to have them repair the roof. As she defended the expense, she explained that "they were very nice young men." She told us that she knew it was all right. "They had such nice manners, and even took me to the bank to get the funds."

The roof repair was minimal at best, and something that should have cost about a third of what she paid. For years, we had been hearing about schemes to defraud the elderly, and figured it couldn't happen to us because, after all, Mama was smart.

But Mama was also Southern, and having good manners counted for a great deal. We didn't realize it at the time, but manners and social skills would become increasingly important to her as her mind began to fail. Later on, they would help her to navigate the confusing world of dementia with a little bit more grace than would have otherwise been the case. We also didn't realize it but we were all in some level of denial. After all, Mama was smart, we would think to ourselves.

After some initial defensiveness about the roofing job, she gradually realized that she had spent too much, and had placed herself in potential danger by relying so heavily on strangers. This was one of the first times that we noticed she was slipping.

Like many with early Alzheimer's, she was lucid most of the time. Until that point, the mental slips and moments of forgetfulness appeared infrequently and with little consequence. However, the roof repair illustrated just how vulnerable she might be. And, how isolated she had become much of the time. It frightened us, and we began talking with one another more about the situation – and our fears.

We wondered if Mama was starting to get senile, and discussed that fear in almost hushed tones. It was like "The Big C." As a culture, we often stutter over words like "cancer," and

"Alzheimer's." It's like, if we say it, then it will happen. That's the big worry, isn't it?

As much as we didn't want to, we began looking more carefully at Mama. We researched Alzheimer's disease. We schooled ourselves in the signs and symptoms of dementia. I know there were times that I felt awful about doing that – like it was some sort of disloyalty.

We discovered that the neighbors were doing most of the grocery shopping for Mother, and that she wasn't going to church as often as she had in previous years. Slowly, she was isolating herself, as is often the case as we grow older. And we discovered that those with dementia, or Alzheimer's, become isolated more quickly, and more completely.

As we worked with Mother over the coming year, we began to see other signs that she was slipping. We began to realize that she really was suffering from dementia, probably Alzheimer's. It was awful to contemplate. And when my brothers and I would talk, we would often ask each other if we were on target. "Is this really happening?" we would ask one another. "Is this what's going on?"

I was very glad that I had a background with consulting in the areas of health and aging, because I knew where to start my research. But even so equipped, I found it difficult. There were days that I felt like Alice in Wonderland, down a rabbit-hole and into another kind of reality. I read everything I could find from the Alzheimer's Association, which was a great resource. I had friends who recommended books, and I started to do Internet research.

My brothers Tom and John were also researching options, such as ways to bring in more supports to her at home. Sometimes when we talked, we felt like we were making progress. Sometimes we felt like we were stuck. We often doubted our own judgment. But as we continued to visit Mother and watch her, we found an increasing number of signs that she was, indeed, slipping. Although Mother never liked to pay taxes, she always worked carefully, and completed tax returns early. Like so many who survived the Great Depression of the 1930s, she didn't like to rely on accountants. She and Dad had developed good files, and a system for handling the multiple tax forms that included investment and capital gains income. How they could manage that, I still can't fathom. But they did. Mother and Dad hated to spend a dime more than absolutely necessary.

However, the time came when Mother's tax forms were scattered all over her desk, along with files that were spilling their contents haphazardly from half-opened drawers, and some that were lying on the floor. Things were much messier than usual, and we noted that was a change. The tax forms were just partially completed, with her name and address at the top, and big zeros at the bottom of the main 1040 form. As we talked with her about the taxes, she explained that she had been very busy, but that she would finish them "soon." She assured us that would be just fine, and that she did not need our help.

Like many of the WWII generation, she avoided discussing her personal finances with her children at all costs. Thankfully, she had forgotten that she'd provided us with Power of Attorney over her finances. My brother John was finally able to get her to sit down and talk with him. She explained that she didn't want to pay the government anything, and shouldn't have to pay the government because she was old, a widow and near penniless.

Actually, she was right on two counts. She was far from penniless.

John persevered once he saw that she had started figuring from the bottom of the 1040 form, where she placed the large zeros. He was able to tactfully intervene to correct the forms and file a return that was more solidly based on reality. We were all very grateful to him, as it would have been quite difficult for us had she been indicted for tax fraud.

As we began looking around the house with a better grasp of reality, we discovered that she had posted dozens of reminder notes to herself. Mother always left herself reminders, but they were few and carefully written, usually close to the phone and her calendar. Now, the notes were posted all over the cabinet doors and countertops next to the phone. They included reminders to do basic things like talk with the neighbor about groceries, feed the cat, bill her piano students, and call the children. And, there were reminders about the reminders. It was a patchwork quilt, and a disheartening discovery.

We also found out she was double and triple billing her piano students, often billing when a family's account was fully paid. Her group of piano students had been slowly dwindling from a high of about 30 students to less than a dozen at that point.

Within a few years, her base of students was to dwindle further to just three stalwarts who remained with her until her retirement party which we gave for her about three years later during the summer. Many of her former pupils came, and it was a delightful validation of her and her work. It was amazing that she was able to continue teaching for as long as she did.

Experts say that people who are musicians, or who play music frequently, are able to maintain their "musical memory" much longer than their regular memory when Alzheimer's hits. This was the case with Mother. She loved music. Playing the piano was one of her passions. She loved to teach, and she was very good. We supported her in her efforts to continue to teach until it became quite clear years later that teaching had become too difficult to manage. In time, we would discover how important music would be to Mother and to all of us as a way to connect when Alzheimer's had ravaged much of her brain. But I'm getting ahead of myself.

At that point in time it appeared to us that, at some level, Mother knew that she was becoming forgetful. But she was fiercely independent, private and committed to continuing with living as she had. She absolutely did not want to discuss anything remotely related to her memory loss. In fact, she denied having any problems whenever we brought up the issue.

She was also fiercely committed to maintaining her independence, and living in her beloved house in Winston-Salem where she had lived with Dad for almost thirty years. But she was also less able to maintain the house.

When we expressed concerns, Mother would make excuses, shift to another topic, or become intensely angry. Mama always lived a bit too close to the emotional edge, and we had learned many years ago to treat her with kid gloves, and watch for signs of an impending emotional storm. We realized that she was very prickly when it came to her living alone, her house and her memory. Often, when we mentioned concerns, she would say things like, "Are you trying to put your old Mother away?" or "You think you know more than your Mother?" "Your Dad would be so ashamed to see you treating me like this." With that kind of response, one does not usually continue the same approach. We began to realize that the direct approach of mentioning our concerns was not a very fruitful one.

We talked less with her about our concerns about her living alone and our worry about her managing her affairs, and more with one another when she was not present. We'd whisper our concerns when we were together at Mother's house. And we talked frequently by phone, sometimes on three-way calls. We began to discuss options and strategies.

We all agreed to visit Mother more often, and scheduled time each month that one of us would visit her and help her out with chores, housekeeping and paperwork. That represented the first of many strategies we developed to help Mother (and us) deal with her Alzheimer's disease.

Being willing to see these difficult changes can be one of the hardest and most heartbreaking of tasks. It's a challenge to face this issue early on, but that's the way it happens. Nobody can prepare you for it. You may have an intellectual understanding of Alzheimer's disease from your experience with other older people, perhaps grandparents or other relatives. You may have had a close friend or spouse who went through this with their parents. It's possible that you know something about the disease from your professional work, as I did.

On one level, that knowledge and experience can be very helpful. On another level, it doesn't help at all. The knowledge and experience helps us later on, after we've come to terms with the fact that Mother (or Dad) has Alzheimer's and will be getting worse. It doesn't help us in the beginning to stare down our denial and our fears – and come to terms with the situation. We watch a parent start to forget things, cling to past skills, stumble over words, write little reminders and we don't want to believe that can be happening.

We don't want to see it for many reasons:

- *It represents a scary reality, with them diminishing before your very eyes;*
- *It means a difficult and painful journey for them and for you;*
- *It suggests a great deal of future caregiving and possibly a financial burden.*

Check things out with friends and family. Read what you can. Start to develop your support system. There are many web-based resources like the Alzheimer's Association, National Council on Aging, as well as national caregiving groups. Local organizations like your local Senior Center can provide excellent information and resources, as well as much needed emotional support. Many faith communities can also provide important support. Check out the Resources Section of my website, Moving Mama, for more information.

www.movingmama.net

Chapter 2: Trying to Make Sense of Things

It is often difficult to spot early changes in memory and behavior because these changes are almost always slow and incremental. Like many people in the United States, the three of us were scattered across the country. Most grown children live at a distance from parents. As a consequence we see our aging parents just a few times a year, if that. Frequently, our parents lament not being able to see us more than they do. If we have children, the laments often increase in proportion to the number of grandchildren around. We feel guilty that we don't have enough time available to visit with them. In our middle years, most of us are busy with careers, caring for growing (or grown) children, and starting to worry about our aging parents. It's one of the givens of our high-tech-fast-paced urban lifestyle. And it can make dealing with a parent's aging issues that much more difficult.

It can take a while to build up a critical mass of information to convince ourselves and other family members that there is a problem. That was certainly the case with us. Until this critical mass is reached, most of us find ways to excuse behavior that doesn't fit, or is difficult to understand. Once family members realize that there is something wrong, we often move into high gear, trying to fix things. Sometimes we blame ourselves, asking "why didn't I see this sooner"?

In truth, it just takes time to realize a family member is having memory problems. And, that's probably a good thing. I wouldn't want someone jumping in to protect me from myself or institutionalize me at the first sign of my failing memory. I'd be long institutionalized by now if that were the case.

With Mother, we visited her more often. We took stock of the state of affairs when we arrived. Was the house clean, or in disarray? Had she been able to care for the cat? Did she have little notes to herself all over the place? Had she fired the housekeeper again? And, we would talk with friends and neighbors to see how they sensed she was doing.

Mama still had a few piano students left, and that was a helpful barometer. We observed how she taught. Her teaching skills remained excellent; she was attentive, resourceful and wonderful with her students. However, she was increasingly unable to handle scheduling and billing. We noticed that she was increasingly confused, and that managing the scheduling and billing was now almost impossible for her. So her base of students began to dwindle to a dozen, and then a half dozen stalwarts. In retrospect, we realized that it was amazing that she was able to continue teaching for as long as she did.

She loved to teach, and she was very good. We supported her in her efforts to continue to teach until it became quite clear a little later that teaching had become too difficult to manage. In time, we would discover how important music would be to Mother and to all of us as a way to connect when Alzheimer's had ravaged much of her brain. But I'm getting ahead of myself.

At that point in time it appeared to us that, at some level, Mother knew that she was becoming forgetful. But, she was fiercely independent, private and committed to continuing with living as she had. She absolutely did not want to discuss anything remotely related to her memory loss. In fact, she denied having any problems whenever we brought up the issue.

She was also fiercely committed to maintaining her independence. She was absolute and unwavering in her decision to continue living in her beloved house in Winston-Salem where she had lived with Dad for almost thirty years. But, it was becoming increasingly clear that she was also less and less able to maintain the house.

When we expressed concerns, Mother would make excuses, shift to another topic, or become intensely angry. Mama always lived a bit too close to the emotional edge, and we had learned many years ago to treat her with kid gloves, and watch for signs of an impending emotional storm. We realized that she was very prickly when it came to her living alone, her house and her memory. Often, when we mentioned concerns, she would say things like "Are you trying to put your old Mother away?" or "You think you know more than your Mother?" "Your Dad would be so ashamed to see you treating me like this." With that kind of response, one does not usually continue the same approach. We began to realize that the direct approach where we would mention our concerns was not a very fruitful one.

We talked less with her about our concerns about her living alone and our worry about her managing her affairs, and more with one another when she was not present. We'd whisper our concerns when we were together at Mother's house. And, we talked frequently by phone, sometimes on three-way calls. We began to discuss options and strategies.

So, what should we do? What can we do?

We continued to gather information and discuss the situation with one another. Each of us also talked with trusted friends whose opinions we valued. Some had already gone through caring for a frail elderly parent. My friend Nancy's Mother was very ill and in need of care, and we would often share stories. Another friend and colleague had lost a Mother years earlier, and talked with me about the grief that comes when facing a potentially long illness.

It makes sense to gather information, discuss the situation and ask for feedback from others who are close to your loved one. Make notes about any changes you observe. Frequently, family members find that their loved one is a bit more forgetful and may repeat things.

People in the early stages of memory loss are also more apt to forget recently learned information. But they usually have excellent recall for earlier memories. Mother's problems with the roof repair, her tax return, billing students and the increase in little notes to herself together indicated memory problems. Any one or two of those issues alone might not point to anything more than normal human frailty. But a growing list of challenges showed a pattern over time for us, and will for you as well.

Early warning signs can also include changes in planning and problem solving skills. People in the early stages of Alzheimer's often begin to show a level of poor judgment that is different from their norm. We saw a reduction in Mother's judgment with her quick decision to have the men fix her roof, and take her to the bank (and the cleaners). In earlier years, Mother would have taken her time to make a decision, checking for multiple quotes, talking with a close friend or her sister, and looking into references. In earlier times, she would not have discussed this decision with her children, so that was nothing new. A number of experts indicate that financial skills are, unfortunately, some of the first to start slipping, so it is wise to be observant to changes in the way your parent manages finances.

*People showing early stages of memory loss may also have trouble
finding the right words, and may start to stumble a bit in speaking,
where this was never a problem before. However, people with an
extensive vocabulary (like my Mother), may be able to find other
words (synonyms) and mask their difficulties longer than the
average person. In fact, Mother's extensive vocabulary allowed
her to mask her dementia with strangers for a long time. When
stumped and unable to remember a word, she would simply
substitute a synonym. Or, in rare cases when that failed, she would
raise her hands and say ... "well, you know."*

I remember when we were talking with Mother during the early
stages of her Alzheimer's disease. A few years before our
conversation about the roof, and before Dad died, the two of them
had gone west to visit my brother John in Wyoming. Then, later
on, after we became concerned about her forgetfulness, she
mentioned something about our growing up in Wyoming.

We corrected her, but she kept to her story, and described in some
detail where we had lived. It appeared that she had juxtaposed a
mental picture of our house in Puerto Rico (where we had lived
growing up) onto more recent memories she had from her trip to
Wyoming. We could not convince her that she was wrong. In fact,
she just became agitated and frustrated with us. Once it is pretty
clear that there is a memory loss, it is usually most helpful to just
go along with the statement or story.

When Mother continued to have problems with her memory, we
decided one of us would go with her to her next visit to the doctor.
At this stage, Mother was still lucid most of the time. She showed
memory loss infrequently, and could often mask her difficulties.
She had excellent social skills, and was able to fall back on them to

successfully hide her memory problems until later in the progression of the disease.

At her visit to the doctor, she was absolutely charming. She was able to win over the doctor, convincing him that she was fine and her children were unduly concerned and overly protective. The doctor deferred to her, and made some sort of inane comments. Mother had given an award-winning performance, and was definitely in rare form. As we got into the car to return home, she smiled and said something like: "Your old Mother is still on the ball, wouldn't you say?" What could we say? We (and the doctor) had been outsmarted, outfoxed and outmaneuvered. She knew it, and we knew it.

It was at this stage that I looked for some resources to help me deal with the very tricky and challenging early stage Alzheimer's that was affecting Mother. *The 24 Hour Day* was one of the first books I read, and I highly recommend it. There were a number of others I also found helpful, including Robert Butler's *How to Care for Aging Parents*. I had met Bob Butler years ago through my friendship with Maggie Kuhn, founder of Gray Panthers, and found him to be extremely insightful with an encyclopedic knowledge of the field.

During this time, I was also on the lookout to find friends and colleagues who had dealt with the issue. As people shared their experiences, it helped me to realize that the trajectory of the disease included many unsettling shifts, where Mother would sometimes appear to be her old self, other times mildly befuddled, and a few times quite confused.

I realized that the ratio of confusion would shift over time, with her becoming increasingly confused and unable to cope. But at the beginning it was very unsettling to find Mother acting like her old self time and again, causing the three of us to wonder more than once if perhaps we weren't jumping to conclusions or being too hasty. Then, she would hit a difficult patch, and we would realize yet again that she was, indeed, declining.

I also realized early on that most adult children experience their own doubts as they confront the disease in a parent. We become angry. I know I was often angry to see Mother with diminished capacity, and the extra load we realized we would now carry. We loved Mama and were totally committed to giving her the kind of care that she gave her Mother. And we were committed to spending what was needed to do so. Even so, I was still filled with anger and grief and self-doubt on a regular basis.

Most of us have periods where we doubt ourselves and our motives. We wish that we could do more and feel pulled between our own needs, our careers, our own families and our parents. It's a tough place. We find we are on an emotional roller coaster, sometimes feeling confident and able to cope, and often feeling overwhelmed. My emotions often ran the gamut of upset or angry to joyful or hopeful – multiple times a day it seemed. I began to understand that very little in my world view, my work or my relationships readied me to cope with and make sense of a senseless illness.

So, get help where you can, from friends and family, community agencies, health and nutrition resources, spiritual networks and faith communities.

Most areas of the U.S. have good local or regional resources to help adults who are caring for an elderly parent. It's important to check out these resources that are available to help family members. I also recommend loading up on books, watching videos, and checking websites,

Look for friends and family members who have lived through a similar experience and talk with them. If groups help you, look into a local support group. And finally, talk with your siblings and begin analyzing your parent's resources and your options. It's never too early to begin looking at what options are available for your parent/s, analyzing community resources, moving to live near or with one of the children, assisted living or nursing home care, caregiving at home, and other options.

Divide up tasks between siblings if you can.

Develop strategies for ways to take care of yourself.

Chapter 3: The Will and The Government

One of the frequent topics of conversation between my brothers and me had become 'what to do with Mama.' We were at the point where we could no longer ignore her memory problems and her growing vulnerabilities. Dad had updated his will before he died, but we couldn't find it. After searching the house and talking over options many times, we all decided that we needed to get her to write a will – and soon.

We had just enough familiarity with the law to know that if Mother's mental state declined much more, it might be difficult to have the will declared valid if we were to run into any problems later. Since I was the next one scheduled to visit, my primary designated task was to get the will completed and signed.

All of the talk about wills had also made me realize that the last will I had executed had also been years before, when I lived in Louisville, Kentucky. It was also time for me to update mine. I purchased one of those legal referral programs that allowed for a certain number of legal referrals to one of their participating lawyers during one's membership year.

I developed my draft and met with the lawyer. It was rather simple, and I had completed my will before going to visit Mama. Somehow, I felt that would give me some extra credibility and ammunition should I need it.

I needed it.

One afternoon when Mama seemed to be alert and interested in talking, I mentioned that I had recently updated my will. "Oh, why did you need to do that? You're still young, and the lawyers just want to get your money," she said. "Oh, Mama. I wanted to make sure that everything I care about is taken care of." She didn't seem impressed. We talked for a bit, and somehow I had an inspiration.

"You know, Mama. A good reason why I did my will is that I don't want the government to get any of my money." She looked at me and said with gravitas, "Well, I don't want the government to get my money either."

"Mother, if something were to happen to me. Say if I were hit by a bus, it wouldn't be right for the government to get my money."

She nodded and said again "I don't want the government to get my money either."

"Not a penny," I said. She nodded and began to ask me more about how I had executed my will. I knew I had hit pay dirt.

I worked on a draft of her will, describing a simple division of assets equally between the three children, as I knew this is what she and Dad had planned for years, and was a cornerstone of the will that Dad had developed. She agreed. I also developed a financial limited power of attorney for John, with the other two of us as back-ups to him if needed. I could tell that she felt good. And she mentioned a number of times being pleased that the government would not get her money.

The next day, I emailed files to the attorney, and had the will professionally prepared. All that remained was to have the will and the limited power of attorney witnessed and notarized. We called her bank, and they set up a meeting for later that day.

As we drove over to the bank, I was both excited and worried. Quite frankly, I was very excited that we were accomplishing this important task, and rather proud of myself, if the truth be told. I was also worried about how Mother would behave, and the potential for some kind of unanticipated difficulty. I could only hope that she would remember what we had done, and would agree to sign the documents in front of the bank officer and notary. And, of course, I hoped that she wouldn't suffer a memory lapse. These had started, and were unpredictable and my worry that accompanied them was to continue to be an issue. It was becoming "the new normal."

I learned then an important lesson that was very helpful to us later as we continued to care for Mama. When she was in a public setting, she was much more agreeable. For years, even as her memory was clearly failing, when she was in a public setting, she found some strength and skill deep within her, and consistently rose to meet many an occasion that would have trumped a weaker person.

As we met with the bank officer, she was on her best behavior. Alert, friendly and talkative, she was stunning. I marveled at her ability to rise to the occasion.

My brothers and I talked about the will and power of attorney a number of times in the subsequent weeks. Sometimes we wondered if we hadn't pushed her a bit too much. And, sometimes we wondered if she really knew what she was doing.

We had to settle for the murky middle ground of mixed motives. We wanted to protect her and us in the event that something happened to her. We knew it would be ridiculous for her to die without a will – intestate. Dad had made a will, which was somewhere, and we had honored his and her wishes, to the best of our abilities. I knew that she didn't want the government to have any of her assets. I didn't want her assets, or mine, in time, so wasted.

Over the coming months, we would place a fair amount of attention on Mama's finances. They had scrimped and saved all of their lives, and had a sizeable nest egg. Dad had made sure to put all of the stocks and brokerage accounts in her name and ours, so that they would transfer upon her death to the three of us in equal proportions, with no tax liability. We wanted to make sure that her assets were preserved for her care, and for us, her children. And since she was losing her ability to manage them, we chose John to step in and help her make decisions. And then to make decisions for her.

When John visited, he would talk with her and help her update her bank balance. This was often difficult because she was unwilling to add any direct deposits as credits. Mother would think she was low on funds. John would carefully explain her income and expenses.

"John, I just don't have any money left."
"You're fine, Mama. You have money in your checking and savings accounts. And in stocks."
"But look at this. Right here," pointing to an erroneous figure in her checking account register
"Mama, your Social Security check goes from the government right to your bank account. It's there. See? "

He would show her the deposit record each time he visited, and she would reply. "But, I never received the check, and I didn't deposit it. So, if I didn't deposit it, then I can't add it to my bank balance."

At least she underestimated her bank balance rather than overestimating it.

Gradually, John quit trying to explain this. And we realized that, with early Alzheimer's, she didn't remember recent events very well.

How do we even begin to tackle helping parents with their affairs? The first and most important thing is to have a plan. If you're lucky, and your parents are now in their sixties or seventies, they may be willing to start planning with you while they are active and very much in charge of their own lives. Today's older adults are more willing to discuss financial and personal issues with their children than were parents of my generation. So you may be able to get a running start on caring for your elderly parents by working with them to find out how they want to handle their affairs as they become older and more frail. That's the ideal. It may or may not be possible in your case, but try to have these conversations if you can. When you're in your forties, see if you can discuss these issues.

My Mother, who was born in 1917, was very much an "old school parent," and did not discuss any of her personal business or finances with her children. So, we were not able to build a plan with her. We had to start where we were able to start, which was when she began to show signs of slipping.

My brothers and I talked by phone and created a very simple plan which we developed over time. The plan was something like this. It's a bit more organized in retrospect than it was as we moved through the process, the value of hindsight.

care as she becomes more frail.

her around the house.

her more often (all three of us).

___ k to see what's happening, track what she needs and what she's able to do (all of us).

- *Do chores and home repairs when visiting (all of us, mainly Tom and John).*
- *Try to bring in help where possible (really tough to do).*

Research options for her future living situation.

- *Investigate assisted living or nursing home options (which I handled).*
- *Put in place some additional support at home with housekeeping and the yard (Tom and John).*
- *Research and discuss home caregiving options (all three of us).*

Protect and manage her assets and her estate.

- *Develop a new will.*
- *Write the new will and have it witnessed and notarized (me).*
- *Write and notarize a limited Financial Power of Attorney for John to handle her financial matters, including banking and brokerage accounts (me).*
- *Write and notarize a Healthcare Power of Attorney so that we could make decisions about her health should she become incapacitated (me).*

Manage her finances.

- *Review her stock portfolio and ensure that the accounts are set up in her name jointly with the three children, with a Transfer on Death option (John).*

- *Review and oversee her taxes to make sure that she isn't filing incorrect information (John).*
- *Track her income and expenses, and manage her major expenses (John).*

This was not nearly as neat and orderly as the list would lead one to believe. It was messy and emerged gradually. However, we did develop the outline of the plan early on. We learned that, although all of the aspects of caregiving were challenging, some were harder than others. Each family is a little different. Having a plan will serve as an important roadmap for this journey.

Anne Hays Egan

Chapter 4: Protecting Her Finances

In retrospect, we realized that we had been very concerned about Mother's management of her finances for over a year before we were able to intervene. John had handled the tax situation brilliantly, and I was able to update her will and put into place a Financial Limited Power of Attorney so that John could begin to handle her brokerage and bank accounts with her.

But it took a good bit of work to be able to manage her finances, and it was a lot of work afterward as well. In the process, we learned a great deal.

The first clue that things were wrong was a change in her financial habits. Mother was one of those children of the Great Depression who managed frugally, and was always in control of her income and expenses. However, as Alzheimer's began to affect her memory, her skills began to slip.

Mother didn't have a lot of expenses. By the time she was in her seventies, the house was paid off, and she had few recurring monthly costs. However, she had a sizeable bank and brokerage accounts which were at risk.

We realized that Mama was not tracking finances well when she began to double-bill her students, and change the way she handled her tax return. And, the roofing fiasco where she spent $12,000 on strangers was a huge red flag for us. At this point, we had already begun to work with her on her will, managing her finances, and putting brokerage accounts in trust.

But when she spent $12,000 on a group of strangers who had come to her door to tell her she needed roof repairs, we moved into high gear. In the late 1990s, there were not nearly as many scams as there are today, but those that existed were frightening.

We had all agreed that John was best suited to the financial oversight task for many reasons. John was the youngest and the peacemaker. Like many families, we had our difficulties and neither Tom nor I would had been comfortable having the other one in charge of Mother's money, but we both trusted John to handle things in Mother's and our best interests.

All three of us supported this plan, and John agreed to keep us informed about her finances and to check with us about any large expenditures. He did that, and we tended to be in agreement about how her money was managed.

One other area where we were in agreement, which was actually rather amazing, was that we talked in general terms about how the money should be spent. And the three of us agreed that whatever funds were needed to be spent for her care would be spent. We were lucky in that regard.

She had taken wonderful care of her Mother, and that example became part of her gift to us, and part of our roadmap. We had grown up with the belief that one takes care of one's parents, no matter what. It's just what is done.

In addition, all three of us have worked in nonprofit, educational and community organizations all our lives and have been steeped in those values. The fact that the three of us agreed to spend what was needed for her care was a miracle, I think.

We weren't dumb, or unaware that she had significant assets at that point in her life. We wanted to spend them wisely to protect what would remain for us. It's just that preserving her estate for us was a secondary, though important, emphasis. How that happened, I don't know.

John kept track of her income and expenses for years. He managed her money wisely, and ensured that funds were well invested to preserve her principal. During Dad's final year when he was very sick with cancer, he had made some unwise investment choices. He held onto his Pan Am stock when the airline was tanking, and that was when we knew that he was in very bad shape.

John started meeting with her broker and researching the stocks in her portfolio. He discovered that too much of her portfolio had been allocated into the broker's own "house stocks," which were basically garbage. Later, the federal government passed a law against this kind of in-house brokerage self-dealing. But, before that, it was a bit wilder.

Gordon G. (not his real name), her broker, was a "good old Southern boy" who had gone to Clemson, pledged a good fraternity, and probably got his job through his family or fraternity brothers. He was not very bright. But, he was very social and visited Mother on a regular basis. She liked him. He was a nice young man.

Once John started managing Mother's funds, he became concerned about this nice young man. John had filed the Financial Power of Attorney with Gordon G., and had talked with him about Mother's portfolio, and soon afterward, Gordon's visits to Mother became more frequent. Probably coincidence.

Although Mama thought Gordon was charming, we couldn't stand him, or what he had been doing to her portfolio since Dad had died.

After talking together by phone, we hatched a plan. We were all going to be at Mother's during the summer, and our plans allowed us to schedule a few days where our visits would overlap. We decided we would schedule an appointment with Gordon. All of us.

John analyzed the portfolio. The three of us looked at other stock and mutual fund performance levels for comparisons. We also talked with Mama's sister Tula and our cousin Carolyn, who was helping Tula with her investments. Tula's portfolio had been managed much more effectively, and it helped to have another "take" on things. Tom and I developed some strategies for the meeting.

On the appointed day, the three of us descended on Gordon's office. Although John and talked with Gordon often by phone and met with him a few times, Tom and I didn't know Gordon very well, but had met him occasionally over the years.

I was the most Southern of the three children, being the oldest and a girl. Having gone to Converse College, I still dressed and acted like a Converse girl. In my day, that meant a certain panache that came with matching clothes, the right jewelry, accessories and shoes. It's a cross I still bear.

My brother Tom was, and is, a big man with a very intimidating presence. John is both friendly and intellectually intimidating. Hell, we all three can be intellectually intimidating when we want to be. And for this meeting, we wanted to be as intimidating as possible.

My role was to start the conversation. So I greeted Gordon in that superficial way that Southern near-strangers of a certain age engage in. Once we had him chatting away, John began to ask questions. Very pointed questions. He went over Mother's portfolio and identified those stocks that had not performed well, zeroing in on the in-house garbage funds.

Meanwhile, looking stern, Tom pulled his chair much closer to the broker's desk, and leaned forward, attentively. Gordon began to flutter and stammer like a schoolgirl. He was clearly unprepared for the level of analysis we had conducted, and the questions we asked. Gordon was not gifted with a great deal of brainpower. He was unprepared, and didn't have good answers. As the conversation continued, he realized that he was in hot water and in danger of losing a preferred customer account.

The conversation ended with John informing Gordon that he was in charge of Mother's account, and that all instructions concerning Mother's investments were to come from him. John provided Gordon with a list of changes that were to take effect. He let Gordon know that he would be managing the account closely, in frequent contact, and would pull the account if Gordon did not handle things more effectively in the future.

We smiled, shook hands and left. Gordon now had his marching orders. I don't know if Mother ever knew that Gordon had been put on notice. But, her account performed much better in subsequent years.

One of the drawbacks to being the peacemaker and best-loved child for John was that he ended up having a tremendous amount of financial responsibility and stress. He willingly shouldered these responsibilities, and was able to manage things amazingly well then, and over the years to come.

We were fortunate in that the three of us agreed about priorities for Mother's care, and we took good care of her money. Actually, we took better care of her funds than we did of own (self-care can be an issue with many of us). If siblings don't agree, or people undercut one another, then developing a plan can be a real problem.

No matter what your parents' financial situation might be, there are things that you will want to do to safeguard their finances, if you can. Again, the sooner you can discuss these issues with your parents, the easier it will be to develop and implement a plan.

There are many more scammers around today than fifteen years ago, when we were dealing with Mother's finances. And scammers are much more sophisticated. They can contact older adults by phone, mail, in person or on the Internet. Some scammers pretend to be government agencies with names and logos that seem quite official. People may call pretending to be a bank representative, someone from Social Security or Medicare, or another official person. The scams are difficult to counter, so the best defense is a good offense. Talk about the issues with your parents. Check with the local Senior Center to see if there are some workshops on how to avoid scams. Do your own research. Talk about situations that you know about, with friends or other family members and remember to share those stories.

There are a number of articles about finances and aging which I recommend. A Google search can put you in touch with New York Times articles, Pew research, the University of Pittsburgh Aging

Institute as well as regular columns on a number of websites. It seems like financial management skills are some of those affected early in the progression of dementia, and the consequences can be devastating.

As money management becomes more difficult for elderly parents, there are a number of things that one can and should do:

1. *Discuss their goals, priorities and preferences as soon as possible;*
2. *Build a plan to protect their assets, working with a financial expert where possible (research options and be careful about vetting your choices);*
3. *Develop a list of important documents and their locations (medical insurance, wills, trusts, advance health care directives, etc.);*
4. *Create limited Powers of Attorney for health care and medical decisions and financial decisions;*
5. *Where possible, protect assets by placing them in joint custody, transfer upon death agreements and/or trusts;*
6. *Research care needs, options and costs and develop plans;*
7. *If possible, purchase long term care insurance or other protective policies;*
8. *If funds are limited, research options such as reverse mortgages, county and state social service and health care programs and other benefits to which a parent may be entitled (local Senior Centers are excellent resources as you begin your search).*

You may find it helpful to consult a professional in a nonprofit such as your local Senior Center that works with the elderly. Do your own research, and please make use of my website, the Resources section of my website, Moving Mama.

Talk with financial and tax specialists if you can, and if the assets are substantial, you will need to take special care to protect these assets from scams, or lapses that come with dementia. It is also important to research how to legally and ethically spend down if assets are limited and parents could qualify for Medicaid at some point.

And review your own potential financial liabilities as well. Adult children have more legal issues and potential liabilities now than was the case in the mid to late 1990s.

When in doubt, talk with others who have cared for an elderly parent and worked through some of the financial challenges. Make sure that the advice you receive is from people that are well informed, and unencumbered by financial self-interest. You want objective feedback from people in the know.

Chapter 5: Standing Up To Others

Mother was raised in the Deep South, and like most Southern girls, she learned her lessons early. By the time she was grown, she had fully internalized the tenets of being "A Southern Lady, "with all of the attendant attitudes, benchmarks, privileges, management skills, and knowledge of accessorizing that are part of that fine art form. She also learned a great deal about how to be tough when situations warranted, standing up for what one believes, and taking charge when needed.

Her Mother was a wonderful artist, often disorganized and forgetful. Gram was also a pragmatist, and a fascinating mix of Edwardian Era culture, early feminism, Unity Christianity, and Women's Christian Temperance Union (WCTU) values. All of these had a significant impact on my Mother.

Race Riots in Guam

Mama worked for the Red Cross as a Club Director during the final years of World War II. After a train trip across the country in 1945 to the west coast, she had an orientation in Honolulu. From there, she went to Guam and then Tinian to run the 'Swabbie Lobby' Club. These recreational clubs were managed by the Red Cross, and scattered throughout the Pacific. Swabbie Lobby was, as the name indicates, for Navy enlisted personnel.

Mother's arrival came just a month or two after a disastrous race riot in Guam, in late 1944. This riot between African American and White military men resulted in deaths and injuries.

Both African American and White Army Airmen came to the Swabbie Lobby Club for food, music, games, skits, reading – and especially for pool. African American Airmen were often the first to drop by the club. The African Americans were almost always given the worst shifts, those that started very early and ended in the mid afternoon. Many would head over to the club to play pool after work.

One day, soon after Mother arrived to run the club, some White Army Airmen came in right before dinner. The pool tables were all taken by African Americans who were engrossed in their games. A number of the Airmen were "Good Ole Southern Boys." As such, they felt entitled and unwilling to wait, especially under those circumstances. They came up to Mama saying "Get those N….. out of here."

Instantly, pool playing stopped. The air was electrified, with an explosion just seconds away. Mother had to have been briefed about the earlier race riot in Guam and the dangerous situation that still existed. But with no hesitation, she moved to stand in between the two groups that were fast forming, and said: " I'm from Alabama, and I know as well as anybody how things are done in the South. But we're on an island in the middle of the Pacific Ocean. And, we're all in this war together."

Mother was movie-star beautiful at that age and spoke with a Deep Southern accent. She was in her late twenties but looked a good ten years younger. She was still nad've about a lot of things, but not all things. Young as she was, she already had that force of personality that characterized her later life.

It was a blend of Southern sweetness and steel. She could claim total control of a volatile situation in a few heartbeats. "I may look young, but I'm older than most of you, and carry a GS rank equivalent of a Captain. I run this club. Both groups will stay. Those are the rules."

They were dumbstruck….It was a knock-out.

The Great, Great Dane

During Thanksgiving of 1965, when we were living in San Juan, Mother took my two brothers and me to St. Thomas for the holidays. I'm not sure what preoccupied Dad at the time, perhaps the aftermath of the evacuation of refugees from the Dominican Republic. Anyway, he was not in the picture. It was Mother and the three of us.

Mama would spend hours researching each site on our itinerary, so that she would know about the area's history, art and culture. And in writing this, I realize that I have developed the same habit, which has greatly enriched my travels.

As was her habit when travelling, we started early and spent our days in non-stop sightseeing. I loved Charlotte Amalie's sights, the harbor and the little stores. Already I had learned the fine art of shopping. The scenery was a breathtaking explosion of tropical color. One of the sights tucked away from most tourists was Bluebeard's Castle. It was on private property, and very nicely hidden at the end of a residential street. Today, it's a boutique hotel.

As we wound our way up a hill filled with large residential homes, we children began to mutter and complain. We had pretty much had our fill of walking, and this appeared to be a "wild goose chase." However, as the tall and partially ruined tower soon came into view, Mother marched ahead, ready for another of her touring conquests.

Then out of nowhere came the largest dog I had ever seen. An enormous Great Dane was leaping over the wall, heading right for us. The size of a small horse (forget pony) the dog was barking ferociously, and would be upon us in just a few bounds. This was one of those times I was so frightened that I literally could not move. I just stared at death on four paws.

Quickly, Mama ran forward waving her arm and pointing at the dog, saying "You stop, right now. Go back. Leave these children alone." Once she got the dog's attention, she continued to reprimand it. The dog slowed down and then stopped. About the same time, a woman came out of the house and began calling the dog by some sort of ridiculous name like "Precious" or "Bumpkins."

Hearing his name and her voice, the dog turned around to face her, and with a faint whimper of recognition, bounded back home. I don't remember ever being so proud of Mother, or so grateful that she was there in full spiritual battle armor looking out for us.

Protecting Her Mama

Gram, our Grandmother was in the hospital in her last few days. Born in 1882, Gram was three months shy of 100 years old, and had lived a rich and full life. Even though managed care was far from its heyday, doctors and hospitals were already expanding their services to the insured.

This practice developed partly because technology was starting to allow hospitals to provide more options for patients, partly a risk-

management measure to avoid lawsuits, and partly to expand
billings and increase revenues. Today, after several decades of this
policy, we find that the greatest medical expenditures for people
are during their last 30 days of life, often due to extensive and
unneeded medical heroics.

Whatever the cause, a very young doctor was trying to talk with
my exhausted and exasperated Mother. He wanted to intubate
Grandmother and put her on a respirator. Mother, the daughter of a
doctor, had her own ideas. She would not stand by to have her
Mother's last days or hours stretched out to a near vegetative state.
Her Father and Mother had instilled in her (and in us) a respect for
the natural cycle of life without the imposition of extraordinary
measures.

The rather clueless doctor was working hard, trying to chip away at
Mother's resolve, using his new-found status as an appointed
medical god (with a little "G"). Finally, Mother had had enough,
and she lambasted the unwitting guy with unexpected fury.

"Now you listen here, young man," Mother said to him, shaking
her finger at him for emphasis and effect. "My Father was a doctor,
with a great deal more experience than you have now at your
tender age. We value life, but we don't believe in these
unnecessary tactics to prolong life, especially at her age."

The doctor was aghast, and continued to press his point. Mother
was unimpressed. "Young man, if this were your Grandmother,
would you suggest that course of treatment? Knowing she's at the
end of her life? A very full life?" She looked down her nose at the
young M.D.

He was backing down, and literally backing off, but she continued to press her point. " I will not stand for any extraordinary measures. I will not allow it. My mind is made up, and you will not change it. Now leave us alone."

The doctor left, but not without first giving Mother a referral slip for a psychiatrist. There were many times we three children felt that sort of referral would have been appropriate and helpful. Just not then. Thank goodness Mother had the strength to prevail against the turkey in the white coat.

Game, set and match to Mother. When she was good, she was very, very good.

Picture Gallery

This picture gallery contains photos of Mama and the family, from 1918 to 1950.

Gram in 1918, with Mama as a baby. Mama's older sister, Tula on the left, and "Sister," the oldest of the children, is on the right.

Mother's Red Cross picture, taken in 1944, when she was 26 years old, before she went to Guam and Tinian with the Red Cross.

Mama with her Red Cross friends, Guam in late 1944. Mama is on the first row, second from the right. Helen Merrill (of Merrill Lynch) was the "house Mother" for the "girls," and is on the far right of the front row.

Mother singing, one of the many performances on Tinian during WW II. They created shows and took most of them on tour.

Here's Mama again with the "Spec Acts," one of her singing groups. She's the one in the middle, clearly on a roll!

Mama made lifelong friendships with a number of the Red Cross women who worked with her on Guam and Tinian, especially the "Spec Acts," Cat, Irma, and Desiree.

Getting ready to return to the U.S. after the war, on an overlook in Hawaii.

Mother and Dad in Montgomery, Alabama in 1950 with me, in her lap.

Chapter 6: Summer Visit to Santa Fe and Travel Challenges

During the spring of 1997, my brothers and I became increasingly concerned about Mother's care. Although I was going to Winston-Salem a few times a year, and Tom and John were covering the other months, we were afraid it was no longer sufficient. We were sharing the management of her care (such as it was), with each of us handling certain aspects.

John was handling her banking, brokerage accounts and taxes. After we updated her will with her, he had Power of Attorney over her financial affairs. He was working on his Ph.D. at the University Kansas, and went to see Mother about every other month. Tom was in Louisville. Both had heavy teaching schedules, but were somehow able to ensure that one of them was with her for about a week every month, with me filling in during spring, summer and winter holidays.

Tom and his wife Ann worked on keeping the house itself in shape. And I worked on revising her will and researching options for her care. The three of us worked as a team, and actually agreed about most things, which I realized in retrospect was a huge gift making everything much easier than it might have been otherwise.

I offered to take Mother for the summer. It seemed like that was only fair, since I had not visited her in Winston Salem as often as had Tom and John. My brothers did need a break. It appeared that I would be able to handle my clients and care for Mother. In fact, I thought she might enjoy the summer music, the opera and the arts. She loved the mountains, and we had plenty of those. We arranged for her to have a check-up with her doctor, to make sure that she could handle the trip. The doctor indicated that, other than the dementia, she was in good health and would be fine to travel and to spend time in the high altitude of the Santa Fe mountains.

In early June, I flew to pick up Mother and bring her back with me to Santa Fe. We had handled the reservations for the return trip for the two of us very carefully, to minimize the time in transit, and to ensure arrival in New Mexico before dark. When we arrived at the airport, we were informed that the flight had been either cancelled or delayed. Mother's Alzheimer's had progressed at this point, and she was suffering from moderate memory loss. We knew that travel would be dicey with the best possible scenario, much less a major roadblock.

My sister-in-law and I demanded to talk with a manager and explained Mother's condition. He made the usual excuses, at which point I used all of the strategies I had learned from Mama to "read him the riot act," as she would have said. Ann and I knew that if we didn't leave then, it would be much more difficult to return to the house only to try and depart again later. It might not happen at all, or with extreme difficulty. We were looking at a window that was fast narrowing, and we needed to take action. We demanded and received a ticket for the next available flight from another carrier, and so began our journey for Mother's summer vacation with me.

We all learned some very important lessons from that exchange with the airline manager. We realized that normal travel inconveniences for most of us become huge life changing obstacles when dealing with a frail parent with Alzheimer's disease. We had spent days, weeks and months preparing for the trip, getting Mother ready and packed. A long wait or reschedule for the next day could have jettisoned all of our plans. We learned that, when necessary, one should demand to speak with a manager and expect reasonable accommodation. We also learned about the importance of having and advocate. By teaming up, Ann and I had greater resolve and capacity than either of us would have had alone.

After we received our new tickets, Ann said to me: "Boy, I would not have wanted to be in his shoes. You were something else." I smiled at Mama, thinking that this set of skills I had learned from her starting at an early age. They were very well ingrained.

Our trip west required a stopover and change of planes in Denver. In fact, it's difficult to fly from the East Coast to New Mexico without changing planes. There were a few options, but most were nonstop from Albuquerque to Atlanta, Baltimore or Orlando. There were no nonstop flights from Winston-Salem to Albuquerque or Santa Fe. So we carefully planned for a little extra time in Denver. It would be a long trip for anyone, much less a frail Mother with Alzheimer's.

The flight went well, and we had a nice dinner in Denver. I had arranged for a wheelchair, which Mother found insulting. However, the walk would have been impossible for her, and she would have been confused by the people-movers that zipped along in the center of the terminals. So, I told Mama that they were offering wheelchairs to many passengers at that point, as part of a training program for new staff, and that it would be very helpful to the airline if she would be willing to help out. In that case, she agreed, and we were off to make our connection.

The woman who was pushing the wheelchair was from Mexico, and she was absolutely wonderful with Mother. No matter what Mother said, she responded in a compassionate and respectful way. Unlike so many, she was not embarrassed or challenged by Mother's dementia and her wild chatter. I thanked her, and talked with her from time to time in Spanish, talking about her move the U.S., her dreams, and letting her know how much I appreciated the way she dealt with Mother. She had made the transition much easier, and I gave her a large tip in gratitude.

The airline policy of boarding people with special needs first was and is a tremendous help. We got Mother situated and thought we would be off. However, there was a delay. For some reason, we waited on the tarmac for long enough for Mother to become distressed and agitated. By this time, it was late afternoon. Mother had not had her nap, and she was tired and becoming a bit difficult, as we all often do when exhaustion hits. She was wondering why we couldn't get going.

"Anne Hays, why aren't we moving?" she asked repeatedly. The flight attendant was wonderful, asking her if she wanted something cold to drink, which she did. But, Mama continued her queries, becoming a bit more upset. When I talked about the plane, she didn't seem to understand. So, I finally hit on a good answer. "Mama. We're waiting for the train to leave the station. The train will be leaving any minute now." She sat back, pleased to finally understand what was happening.

A man sitting nearby gave me a number of nasty stares. I didn't have any insights into his concerns or his psyche. But, it appeared on the surface that he was bothered by Mother's constant banter, her worry, and my very creative answer. I thought, as I looked at him following one of his nasty stares: "Look, jerk. It worked. She has Alzheimer's. Give it a rest. Hope you get the opportunity for hands-on learning yourself someday." And so forth.

Finally, we arrived in Albuquerque, both exhausted. As we began to de-plane, the flight attendant mentioned to us that a wheelchair was waiting for Mother. To which Mother replied, "Oh yes, she had one of those for me before. But, I'm not nearly as old and frail as she thinks," and she winked and smiled at the flight attendant as she walked off with a flourish. The flight attendant and I had a

56

moment where our eyes connected, and she seemed to say "Good luck." It helped.

We had a nice ride up to Santa Fe, and Mother loved seeing the mountains in the early evening light. She was treated to her first of two beautiful sunsets over the Sangre de Cristo Mountains that encircle Santa Fe. Once we arrived at my house, we had dinner. She played with the cat and we talked about Santa Fe. She played my piano a little, and then we both turned in. It had been an exhausting day. And the days to come were to be even more stressful.

The next morning, I awoke refreshed and ready to go. Mother was still sleeping, so I tried to keep quiet. But, after a few hours of intermittent checking on her, I finally brought her some breakfast. She woke extremely dizzy and was not able to keep anything down. She went back to sleep. I called my friend, Beth, who was a nurse. She recommended I keep an eye on things, try to get her to eat, and to call her back if Mother didn't improve. After repeated attempts, trying a number of things, I began to worry that she might not be getting enough oxygen or liquids, and that she could become increasingly dehydrated.

After some effort, I was able to get Mother dressed, but she went back to bed again, saying "I'll feel better soon. I've just got such a woozy head. Do you have any smelling salts?" Fortunately, I found some, and they helped a little, but not much. She still had eaten very little since early last evening, and had very little to drink. She lay back down again.

I called Beth again. She said that she and her husband would come over and help me get Mother to the hospital emergency room. Beth and Chris were wonderful. A few minutes later, she and her husband arrived. We tried to get Mama to walk between us, but she was stumbling. Beth's husband, Chris said to me, "She's so small, I can carry her." And, to Mother, he asked "Do you mind if I carry you to the car?"

Waving one hand as if she had a lace handkerchief, she smiled as he was picking her up. Never one to miss an entrance or exit, she said "Oh, my. You're so strong….. such a nice young man." Off they went, with Beth and me in tow.

At the hospital, we discovered that her oxygenation levels had dropped to the high 80% level, so she was given oxygen there and a prescription for an oxygen tank. Relieved, we all packed her back up and took her back home. Soon, we were equipped with a portable oxygen tank, and I began to think we had solved the problem.

Not so.

Later, when I went in to check on Mother, she had taken off the oxygen tube. I started to fix it for her and she complained, "Oh, Anne Hays, I can't stand this. It scratches my nose. It's awful." As I explained how important it was for her to use to breathe, she seemed to understand and agreed to wear it. She lay back down. After a few more minutes, I checked on her again. She was napping comfortably, without the oxygen. This went on for a few hours. I would fix it, and she would take it off. I finally realized that, with her dementia, she would probably not be able to remember to keep the oxygen tube attached. Consequently, her blood oxygenation would drop, and she would continue to have altitude sickness.

I called both brothers and explained what was happening. We all agreed that Mama would probably not do well in Santa Fe after all. We planned for me to return her back home. We were able to book a flight the next day. Fortunately, I was able to keep her hydrated, oxygenated and fed enough that she was able to avoid becoming dizzy and ill again. And, so she was able to travel the next day.

I called the airline and spent quite a bit of time setting things up so that someone would meet the car with a wheelchair while I took the car to short-term parking and came back around. That was not to be, and the departure turned into a circus.

Once we dropped below the 7,200 foot elevation of Santa Fe, Mama started to feel a bit better, which was a good thing since she continued to remove her oxygen tube. But, even though she was feeling better, she was still weak and would not be able to walk more than a few steps. I thought that the pre-arranged wheelchair would solve that problem. I arrived, but the wheelchair was not there. Thus started a very challenging trip to return Mother back home. Once at the airport, she quickly became tired, and the trip was long, difficult and confusing for her. It was for me, too.

I was both relieved and upset to be returning Mama back home. We had done everything we could to check out the trip beforehand, including a conversation with her doctor. But I still felt somewhat guilty for not being able to care for her as well as my brothers had done, and felt somehow responsible for the "failed summer trip."

Later, I was to realize that many medical professionals are quite limited in their understanding of how high altitude affects the elderly, especially those that have lived their lives at sea level. They are equally challenged when it comes to discussing a frail elderly parent's condition and limitations. Things are better now than they were in the mid to late 1990s, but the health care system needs a great deal of improvement if we are to effectively address the growing challenges facing this next group of older adults now retiring. Baby boomers like me.

That experience, and many others like it, taught me to always do my own research in addition to checking with medical professionals, financial and legal advisors, and others. It also taught me to have a support system in place that I could depend upon when the inevitable surprises would come my way. In this case, my brothers were expecting to have a summer off and I was not anticipating Mother's serious altitude sickness. We were able to manage the changes because we had support networks in place and we were willing to be flexible. I spent additional time with Mama in Louisville, and my brothers and sister-in-law pitched in.

Oftentimes, a friend who has recently cared for an elderly parent can be a Godsend. My friend Nancy's Mother had died a few years before, and she was in a position where she could talk about the challenges and the good times with a bit of objectivity. Her stories buoyed me, and gave me perspective. I talked with a number of other friends and often with my two brothers. This helped us to think about different options, consider new strategies, and get support for the stressful work of caring for an elderly parent.

From this and so many other experiences with Mama, I learned to plan as well as possible, develop supports, and be ready for the unexpected. Expect it!

It can be so frustrating to spend hours developing a plan for some area of an elderly parent's care, only to find the plans go up in smoke, as mine did! I was frustrated and angry. Later, I realized that we all did the best we could with the information we had. The doctor indicated that even with Mother's history of lung problems, she would be fine in Santa Fe. The problem was, the doctor didn't really know what he was talking about. He didn't understand the impact of high altitude living on elderly people. Many elderly people find that they cannot handle the thin air at Santa Fe's almost 7200 feet above sea level. What can you do?

Plan as best you can. Research any area related to travel with or moving a frail elderly parent. Talk with others who have encountered similar situations.

Then develop a back-up plan. One thing you can count on is that some of your plans won't work – for all kinds of reasons. It's part of what makes caring for an elderly parent frustrating and sometimes scary. We really are not in control much of the time.

Try to limit the number of variables you must deal with. Give yourself plenty of time, and add extra time on top of that just to give yourself a bit of "wiggle room." Build in some supports for yourself so that you can take care of yourself while you're also taking care of your Mother, Father, spouse or other loved one. And, if you realize you're caught in a bind, ask for help.

Anne Hays Egan

Chapter 7: Hiring, Firing and Blowing Smoke

As we began to spend more time with Mama, we realized that she needed additional help at home to manage day-to-day chores. For some time, we had continued to keep the yard man that Dad had hired years ago. Since she knew him and was comfortable with him, Mama was fine having Bill come to work in the yard. She had help in the house for many years, but for some reason, there had been nobody to help out for a number of years after the last housekeeper had left. And, of course, nobody could really fill her shoes according to Mama.

So, we decided to "help" Mama by hiring a housekeeper. The first few times we hired someone, she acted as if she were in full agreement. Someone would be hired to come in to clean and make sure that Mama was all right. But anyone we hired was gone within a month or two. Nothing we tried seemed to help.

For someone with diminished mental capacity, Mama was extremely clever when she wanted or needed to be. Mother would say something like "Oh, I'm not sure what happened. I think she got another job," or "I'm all by myself. I don't have to have someone to clean up after me. It's a nuisance." She would often complain that it was too expensive and that she just didn't have that kind of money anyway.

About money. As adults who came of age during the Great Depression, they were so tight with their money, it sometimes screamed in protest. The feeling of not having enough permeated their psyches, and they passed along some of that to the three of us.

The truth was that the two of them had lived frugally all of their lives, scrimping, saving and investing wisely. When we were growing up, we hardly ever went out to eat, and when we did it was usually the occasional trip to Morrison's Cafeteria after church. Mother sewed her clothes and mine to save money. She loved it. I hated it. I wanted the clothes with the labels. The Villagers and the sweaters with the ribbons down the front of them. The Weejuns.

They liked the "Blue Light Specials" at Kmart. They splurged little, but when they did it was on a nice house in a good neighborhood They saved for our college funds, for music lessons and concerts, books, and travel. Over the years, they had managed very well.

Now, in her old age, Mother had a very nice nest egg. Not enough to live a wanton high life. But more than enough to cover her needs.

However, the financial fears and frugality were so deeply ingrained that she knew no other reality. In fact, we realized later that as her grasp of reality slipped in her final years, she lived in fear of impoverishment. Getting her to accept help was an uphill battle at best.

My brother John, the one who visited most often, was tasked with making sure she was able to manage the house, and working to schedule supports like a housekeeper. So, when he met with the next prospective housekeeper, he made sure to explain to Mama the importance of having this help around the house. He thought, with extra time and conversations, that she understood that she could afford and deserved this expenditure.

It appeared she had deferred to his wishes. When talking about it later, he remembered that she smiled and told him how much she appreciated our concern. "You are so good to me, but you worry too much. Your old Mother has been taking care of herself for a lot longer than you have, you know."

Left handed compliments were her specialty. She also specialized in appearing to defer to others. But, she hardly ever did that. She liked being in control, especially as control over her own world was slipping. She was very crafty and knew how to get her way, as do many Southern women.

Mama explained: "The neighbors are like family. They take me grocery shopping and sometimes to the mall. Louise picks me up for church. And I still drive some, you know. Not on the big roads, but to get music and so forth." Her comment "and so forth" would become one of the many expressions she would use more often over time to mask her diminishing vocabulary.

A very deep bond had formed between Mother and the couple next door some years ago when their teenager was a baby. Mary had gone back to work and had someone fulltime looking after the baby. The child care worker was not to take him out anywhere in her car, but she did. And Mother noticed. She told Mary about the lapse. They were like family after that.

Not only were the neighbors incredibly helpful to Mother during the last few years, they provided us with updates on her condition, and how they saw her coping. They also provided Mother with a great smokescreen she used often with us when she felt we were interfering too much (which, unfortunately, was often). She'd let us know that they were always around, grocery shopping and helping out with little things that were now too difficult for her to handle.

When we could, we'd hire people for a short while, and then Mama would fire them. That became ritualized into a dance that occupied a fair amount of all of our time until we realized that we could let certain things slide. Following repeated failures, we stopped putting so much effort into the task of finding her a housekeeper.

We were to learn that caring for an elderly parent with Alzheimer's required constant prioritizing, along with a willingness to let go of those things that could be postponed, that were not critical. Those skills became lifelines for us later on.

We were also worried about Mama's driving, especially after she told us that she only used the car for short trips, like to the music store, always avoiding "the big roads." The big roads, we discovered, referred to the two interstates that bisected Winston Salem. She had never liked driving on the interstate, but had not called it "the big road" until after we noticed her problems with her memory.

We were to learn many times over the years that, in spite of the gradual diminution of her mental capacity, her ability to take control and to do things her way was not diminished in the same way. In fact, she may have become a bit more committed to getting her way, as one method of controlling her world which was fast becoming much more confusing.

Her driver's license was coming up for renewal. Naively, we thought that, with her memory problems, she might not even notice the license expiration date. We figured she would simply let her license lapse.

We were wrong. She definitely noticed, and she was determined to keep her license. Again, this represented an important part of being an independent adult. She told us not to worry, that she would handle things. And handle them she did.

Mother contacted Louise, her friend who took her to church. She asked Louise to take her to get her license renewed. There were so many times when Mother was confused about her music schedule, or billing, or her bank balance. But, she knew she needed to renew her license, and it was a priority for her.

Louise and my brother John were quite close, so she called him to tell him about the license renewal. Interestingly, Mother had not mentioned this to any of us. As Louise and John talked, they both figured that Mother would fail the test, and that would be the end of that. So nobody was really worried about Mother's driving at that point.

A few days later, Louise called John in hysterics.
"You would not believe what your Mother did this morning, she said."

John was afraid that perhaps there had been a scene, or Mother had become upset at not having her license renewed. But that wasn't it at all. Louise explained that Mother had been dressed and ready to go when she arrived to pick her up. And Mother arrived at the Motor Vehicle Department battle ready.

With the skill of any hardened general, Mother had planned her attack and executed her strategies brilliantly. She chatted up the man who was giving her the paper and pencil test, flirting and telling him how smart he was, and asking for definitions to some of the questions.

Even with early Alzheimer's, she had still managed to outfox the clerk and get him to give her answers to many of the questions without his having any idea he was doing that.

"I couldn't believe it," said Louise. "Here she was, just talking away, and getting one answer after another. When I picked her up, I could tell she was ready for that test. She was really something else. And she knew exactly what she was doing! In fact, she said to me as we left, 'Now wasn't that just the nicest young man'."

John and Louise had a good laugh, and then he called me and our brother Tom to give us the bad news: Mama still had a valid driver's license. In our next phone conversations with her, she let each of us know that, "yes, of course I got my license renewed. "

She crowed a bit, and was quite pleased with herself, if the truth be told. She had a right to be proud. She had emerged victorious this time in one of her many little battles with her brain.

We realized we needed to do something to keep our eyes on her driving, and try to get her to either not drive or to limit her activities. But she would change the subject often when we discussed driving. We began watching the odometer on her car. It didn't move. For months, it didn't move.

We'd ask her about driving, couching our questions in not so cleverly disguised queries about how well the car was performing, and whether it needed any maintenance work. She would almost always respond by saying something like "It's just fine. I don't drive that much. But, it's a good solid car."

In fact, for most of that year, the odometer showed no movement. So, after a while, my brother John decided to remove one of the spark plugs to keep her from driving. We were all afraid that driving once in a great while would be much more dangerous than not driving at all. And, having the car not start could serve as an important barrier to driving without impinging upon her sense of independence. We felt like real cheats, but, it seemed like the right thing to do.

So we removed a spark plug. Mama never talked with us about not being able to start the car. And, we never mentioned driving to her again.

We realized later that she felt so much more comfortable and in control by having a current driver's license, and a car in the garage. Never mind that she never used the car any more. It was a symbol. And at some level she was sharp enough to realize both that she needed the symbols (the license and the car) – and that her driving could be dangerous for her, and could get her into difficulty. She was both smart and savvy.

But what we did not see at that point was her gradual withdrawal from others. She went to church less often. She had been sick, so we thought the change was due to her health. However, as time went on, she went to church less and less.

For years, she had been a leader in the church, active with Presbyterian Women and other groups. But, her connections waned and she began to make excuses. "Well, last Sunday, I was just tired," or "You know, it's not the same." or even "Perhaps I'll go next week." Even when Louise would offer to come and pick her up and sit with her, Mother made one excuse after another.

She became increasingly unwilling to engage in social activity, especially on a large scale like a church service. Louise began coming over a bit more often to visit with Mother and talk about church activities, which she enjoyed a great deal.

Music had been, and continued to be, a large part of Mama's life. Even after she had retired from teaching, she still played the piano every day. She played well, and practiced her favorite pieces faithfully. There was little change evidenced in that sphere of her life. And she continued to look for new music for her students that would supplement *John Thompson Book Three* and Golliwog's *Cakewalk* and other pieces I can't remember.

Mama had been the president of the local chapter of the Music Teachers Association, but by this time she had few contacts with that network. She had a very few students, three I think, who she taught most weeks until the late 1990s. She practiced and played for her own enjoyment. And she talked about music with her sister, Tula, who taught piano as well as violin.

A parent with Alzheimer's disease provides grown children with many surprises. The trajectory of the disease is like a sailboat tacking across a large body of water in variable weather conditions. There is a great deal of change in one's condition and in one's ability to navigate.

Sometimes, the parent surprises us with their skill, abilities and acuity as Mother did with the trip to the Motor Vehicle Bureau to get her license. We would have never imagined that she could have passed the test. And, she wouldn't have passed without the unwitting help of "that nice young man." We found it to be hysterically funny, and quintessentially Mother. And she was extremely proud of herself.

Then there are always those times when we discover that things are not going well. We discover new areas of loss, and new challenges.

We saw Mother becoming increasingly confused with handling finances, her billing and her taxes. We discovered that she was becoming increasingly isolated and alone. And, there was not much we felt we could do, except to visit more often and work to try to build a support network around her.

When one solution failed, like hiring housekeepers, we had learned to let go of our plans and regroup, or try other ideas. Helping Mother deal with life as she began to lose ground required all of the creativity we had.

This was as true for Mother as it was for the three of us. There were things that made us laugh and difficulties that we found sad and disheartening. It was difficult to see someone who had a razor sharp mind become increasingly befuddled and unable to cope.

That was probably why Mother was so proud of herself in getting her driver's license renewed. It was a triumph.

Dealing with the disease was also exhausting. My brothers and I talked with one another often, increased our visits to her, and helped her with an increasing workload. We noticed the toll that the additional activity brought, but what we didn't see until later was the stress created by having a loved one with Alzheimer's. She struggled, and we all struggled with her.

We were also beginning to talk about the future, and the options that might exist for her care when she became increasingly unable to cope. But we knew that was still in the future.

The not too distant future.

Chapter 8: Considering Options for Her Care

After many months of visiting Mother, taking care of her business affairs, and trying to ensure her comfort and safety, we realized that we were slipping the wrong way down an increasingly sharp incline. In short, we were not maintaining. We were losing ground.

Things were getting tougher and more complicated. We were not going to be able to keep helping her from long distances, each of us visiting her once a month or so.

We faced numerous problems.

We had discovered some time before that soon after we would put supports in place, like a housekeeper, she would let them know gently but firmly that she didn't really need them. She just didn't want the help we arranged. If Mother had been willing or able to allow people to come in to help, we would have been able to manage better from long distances. But, as it was, we were all afraid that any moment, we would get a call from Mary or Louise saying that Mama had fallen, or gotten lost, or had some other problem that came from living alone.

Mother was increasingly isolated, and seldom left the house. She was losing touch with people who had been friends for decades. Thank goodness she had Mary and Baird next door, Louise from the church, Tula and her three children.

She became increasingly afraid that she was near penniless. She didn't want to spend any money. We would reassure her that she had sufficient assets, which just made her laugh at us. So John continued to manage her finances, taking on increasingly greater responsibilities, and working carefully to try to handle things as

Mother would have herself years before, when she had her mental faculties more intact.

We could see that Mama was coming to depend much too much on her dear friends and neighbors, Mary and Baird. We, and they, found we were all concerned about that, and John talked frequently and honestly with them about mutual concerns, and options.

Like so many middle aged children who find themselves as caregivers for an elderly parent, we discovered that we had "backed into" the caregiving roles. We had not expected to be traipsing to North Carolina on a regular basis to provide caregiving to Mother. But, that was what happened, and that's usually the way most people find themselves caregiving as elderly parents become increasingly frail.

We found that there just weren't enough hours in the day, or enough days in the month to do what we knew had to be done. Thankfully, Mother had a nice-sized nest egg, so we were able to pay for a few services – that is, when she would allow that to happen.

At that juncture, it became clear that before very long, the task of caring for Mother would become impossibly large for the three of us. John and I lived in the West, a good day's trip by plane; and Louisville was a long day's drive for Tom and Ann.

We were each afraid in our own way that something bad could happen to Mother. It didn't matter that she refused a lot of the help that had been offered. We felt individually and collectively responsible for her. Increasingly responsible as her skills diminished. And, we were starting to face a sort of anticipatory guilt for something that might go wrong. It was, quite frankly, an awful feeling.

As the eldest, I have often found myself raising issues with my two brothers when we needed to discuss family matters. And this was no different. I talked with each brother separately and together. When I brought up my concerns about Mother's care, they agreed that she was fast becoming frail and forgetful, and we could all see a time soon when she would not be able to remain in her house alone.

Over the months, I began researching nursing homes and discussed my findings with my brothers. It seemed like the best choice to me at the time, but neither of them were ready to move forward with the decision. They did not want to place her in a facility. In retrospect, I'm glad that my initial suggestions met with resistance. They were right. We found that out later on when Mother was in a rehabilitation facility for about a month, when she drove the staff to distraction with her repetitious questions and demands.

It's not easy trying to figure out how to care for a frail elderly parent. For one thing, they have their own priorities. Most need to remain as independent as possible. I imagine I will be resistant to efforts for caregiving and making decisions for me when I reach that age. Mother, with her own unique personality, was especially resistant to our efforts to help. She actively resisted our best intended suggestions much of the time.

And, in some cases, it felt like we reverted to our feelings when we were children - - hiding some of the things we were doing that we knew Mama didn't like, and telling tales in order to stay out of what we expect will be trouble.

But we also found that, even when we were thrown back to those times of feeling like children misbehaving, our roles had very much reversed. We found ourselves uncomfortable parenting our parent, wanting to do the right thing, and feeling incredibly stressed and ill prepared to do so.

Like others going through similar situations, we stumbled along our way to solutions. It was messy. We made a lot of mistakes. We had a lot of successes.

Gradually, as we talked about the challenges, we began to see what would not work more quickly than what would work. And we kept muddling along.

After some time, we realized that we could think of a nursing home as an option, but not the only option. We shared stories and compared notes. Over a period of six to nine months, we handled things by increasing our number of visits, developing a list of things that needed our attention, and dividing up tasks.

Finally, at Christmas that year, we sat down late one evening after Mother went to bed to talk about what in the world we should and could do.

We knew that, although there were a number of options, there were really only a few practical alternatives to consider.

- We could try to put her in a nursing home, but the good ones had long waiting lists, and the costs were high. We knew she would blow her stack at the mere thought of being "put away," and that was not pleasant to contemplate.

- We could leave her in Winston Salem, but we knew that she would probably have some type of accident or incident – and sooner rather than later.

- We realized that we could have a competency hearing and have one of us declared as her guardian. But she was still sharp enough some of the time to realize what was happening, and we knew that would break her heart.

Quite frankly, the options all looked rather grim. It was hard to think about what to do next at that point. We were tired, and extremely stressed. And it was turning out to be a hard Christmas that year.

When caring for an elderly parent, most of us face times during the journey when we feel absolutely overwhelmed, stressed, out of control and helpless. It seems like, whatever the challenge, it is intractable. It can't be solved. It requires more of us than we can give. It is an absolutely devastating place to find oneself in such a place. And most of us find ourselves in that place at least once during the time we care for our elderly parents. Most of us encounter this multiple times.

So, what can you do? I'll outline some things that we discovered helped, and point out a number of resources that can be of assistance to you no matter what your particular situation. Having a plan helps. When we're up against a wall, being able to refer back to a plan is important. A plan serves as an anchor.

Taking time to take care of yourself is critical. Even if you feel like you don't have five minutes to spare, then give yourself four minutes of peace. Meditate for a few minutes if you can. Take deep breaths. Try to give yourself some small gifts of healthy things –

time with a friend or family member who lifts your spirits, a favorite book, a walk outdoors, a date night with your spouse or partner. Whatever feeds your soul.

Remembering that this is tough for everyone – you, your siblings and your parent. You're all in the soup together. It won't last forever. The crises will come, and they will go.

Prioritizing, and clearing the decks – when times are especially tough, do only what you must. Prioritize your "to do" list and remove anything that isn't essential. It can be dealt with later.

Getting support from friends, family members, others who have gone through what you're facing, or an Alzheimer's support group. People in Alcoholics Anonymous have discovered a wonderful secret that keeps people sober for years. That is, what's too hard for any one of us isn't too hard when you can share it with the group, and get support. Be cautious about what you disclose until you know the group, and be sure that what you may share in confidence is shared with someone who can keep confidences. Support groups have grown exponentially over the years, and they've helped thousands of people. Check with your local or state Alzheimer's Association or Senior Center.

Getting practical support for caregiving is often essential. It's not only the mental and emotional stress, but the sheer workload that can be overwhelming. Sit down with your siblings or other caregivers who are part of your core support team. Identify the tasks that need to be handled, how they're being handled now, and what needs to be done in the near future. Talk with others who have gone through this caregiving experience for their ideas and suggestions.

Go to the Alzheimer's Association website, as well as others, such as the National Council on Aging, National Caregiving Association, and my website, Moving Mama. Talk with someone at your local Senior Center. You will probably find some new resources you didn't know existed, services that can be scheduled, local respite care programs, or volunteers who might be able to help out.

It can be very difficult at times, and much can be managed by using some of these tools mentioned above. And if you'd like, please share your own experiences, and tools you've found helpful on my website.

Anne Hays Egan

Chapter 9: Striking Out and Striking a Bargain

As we moved into the next year, we found that Mama continued to be stubborn about any questions we posed that related to her health, her house, or her independence. That, of course, covered a lot of ground.

Mama had become stubborn about a number of things. Actually, a lot of things. She was never known for her flexibility, and as she struggled with her memory and her fading independence, she became absolutely mulish. When we mentioned we were concerned about her living alone, she would stop the conversation by telling us to change the subject. Sometimes, she would just walk out of the room in a huff.

Mother could still make a dramatic exit when needed.

Feeling in a bit of a quandary, we decided we'd call Mother's sister Tula and talk with her about the situation. We hoped that Tula would have her usual calming effect on Mama. We also hoped somewhat naively that Tula might be able to convince Mama that we were very concerned and were actually trying to help (not punish) her.

So one evening, we called Tula. It started out as a nice conversation, catching up with one another and trading stories. Southern families love stories, and Gram's branch of the tree was full of storytellers, including Mama, Tula and many of their children.

After a while, the conversation turned to our concern about Mama, and things went downhill faster than a world class skier. One minute we were chatting, and the next minute, Mama laid into us, giving us no quarter.

"So, you think your old Mother is crazy?"
"No, Mama," and "No, Lorene," We all said in unison.
"I'll have you know I've lived a lot longer than you children and I know a thing or two. So, you just hush up."
"Now, Lorene. They love you. They're just trying to be helpful," said Tula.
"Tula, you don't know what I have to deal with. They're trying to put me away. I won't have it."

At this point, the conversation had become a shooting match with Mother lined up against the four of us. Though she was outnumbered, she was still in clear command. She was intimidating in spite of her cognitive impairment. Tula assured her that she loved her, and that she knew we meant well.

We all apologized and got off of the phone as soon as possible.

Poor Tula was a wreck, I found out in a quiet call made soon afterward to check on her and to apologize for putting her in the middle of things. We worked hard not to do that again, and asked for her help in a big way only one more time later on.

Mother, on the other hand, was on a tear. She stormed around the house in a full tirade. She accused us of calling her crazy, of not minding her, and many other things. Basically, we all sat in the kitchen with our heads down, trying not to agitate her further, and waiting for the storm clouds to subside. They finally passed, but only after a time.

Just as she did when we were children growing up, Mother informed us that although she was very upset with our behavior, she still loved us in spite of the terrible treatment we'd dished out. We said good night. Everyone kissed and made up, and Mama went upstairs to bed.

We, on the other hand, remained down in the kitchen, whispering about the situation and wondering what in the world we would do. We had discussed the options before. Many times.

No one of the options was good. But this time, we knew that we had finally come to the point where we had to do something. She wasn't safe alone any more. And she didn't want to do anything we suggested, either. So we were really stuck.

It felt absolutely awful. This time was probably one of the low points for the three of us. We felt at a terrible impasse. We were exhausted, angry and upset.

We had done our homework and were ready to take some actions that would protect our Mother if we absolutely had to do that. But we simply could not think about taking this situation to have us court ordered to be her guardians. It's hard to feel that helpless. In addition to feeling helpless, we were all growing increasingly angry at Mama and at the situation. Her resistance was due only partially to her Alzheimer's, and to the normal desire not to lose independence. She had a long history of bad behavior. She could be a drama queen and a willful, intransigent bitch when she felt threatened.

We were stuck in a very difficult stalemate.

We also felt very much afraid as we confronted the situation.
Afraid for her. Afraid for ourselves. All three of us are teachers
and researchers, so we place a great deal of stock in studying an
issue and talking about it. We do love to talk. So, we did.
I went upstairs to check on Mama, to make sure she was in bed.
My brothers remained in the kitchen talking in "sotto voce." For
the first time I could remember, we were beginning to lose heart.
We were afraid that we might have to take legal action to have
Mama declared incompetent if we could not find a way to move
her to a safer place, closer to one of us or to bring in some serious
supports for her at home in Winston.

However, before going to bed, she had "read us the riot act" prior
to the kissee-kissee forgiveness and making up which so
permeated our lives from the time we were little too long after we
were grown. She had let us know in no uncertain terms that she
would not consider moving. She was still angry following the
lengthy phone call with Tula. She didn't remember a lot of what
happened recently, but she could often remember what was most
inconvenient for us. And this conversation, she remembered very
well.

"I don't know what we're going to do," I said to my brothers.
"This is terrible,"
"It doesn't look good," they replied.

We talked for a long time about our options. We were concerned
that trying to get conservatorship in North Carolina, when none of
us lived in the state. We feared it could be a lengthy and expensive
process. We were concerned that she might find a way to rise to
the occasion once again and, though she was much less able now
to "pass for normal," she could still surprise us. We realized that, if

we prevailed, it would break her heart and ours. And it would probably break her spirit.

Even though she had considerable memory loss, she did remember certain things, and she would probably understand part of what was happening to her. We were concerned that it could throw her into a rage, and off of an emotional cliff. We shuddered at the thought of what legal action would do to her and to us. We feared that we didn't have the strength to face something that would undoubtedly be ugly at best.

Like so many adult children caring for a frail, elderly parent, there were many times when we felt overwhelmed by the enormity of the tasks. And this was definitely one of those times. There did not seem to be any good options. Only varying levels of difficulty and challenge. So, we decided we'd think about it and continue talking.

Something happened as we talked that can only be called grace.

As we continued our discussion, an idea began to hatch. One of us, probably Tom, came up with a plan that struck all of us as a wonderful, creative, and rather daring solution. This was breakthrough thinking that represented the only decent alternative we could find.

Tom proposed that we talk with Mother about how much he and his wife Ann wanted her to visit because they hadn't seen as much of her as they would like. He suggested we all talk with her about how they needed her to visit, and needed her help. We could use this story as a ruse to get her to Louisville, and in a safer, more supervised situation.

85

We spent some time talking through the strategy. Over the next few days, it continued to take shape. It morphed from an initial idea of a long winter visit to a potential move for Mother. We decided we would look to see if we could find some property very close to Tom and Ann's we could purchase for Mother.

Ann was a real estate broker, and a great help to us in looking at options. Since we had Mother's Financial Power of Attorney, we could purchase property.

Meanwhile, we decided we would plant the seed, and talk with Mother about visiting Tom and Ann.

There were a number of times at the beginning that we felt a bit guilty about this level of subterfuge. After all, we were planning to move her from her home in Winston-Salem where she had lived for over 25 years to the new place in Louisville. However, the neighbors who had been like children to Mother had been talking with us about Mother's recent declines. And they were increasingly uncomfortable with being Mama's "go to" help in times of need. They were doing more for Mama that was appropriate, even for very close friends who were almost like her children.

As Mama's health and memory continued to slip, it caused them, and us, great concern. They were both medical professionals and were very worried about her continuing to live in the house alone, for all intents and purposes. We also knew that we didn't have many other choices. The options we had been discussing for months didn't work. The only thing that now made sense was this new, creative plan that had seemingly come to us "out of the blue."

At some deep gut or psychic level, I knew that this strange idea to move Mama was our answer. It was the way out of our impasse.

So we agreed that our subterfuge was the best, and kindest, choice. But, it was not an easy one.

We then began talking much more specifically with Mama about this trip. The four of us discussed, reviewed and re-reviewed our agreements and strategies, making sure we were all on the same page. We looked at dates. And we talked with Mama, emphasizing how much Tom and Ann wanted and needed her to come to visit.

To our joy, Mama became interested in making this trip to visit Tom and Ann.

We learned a very important lesson from that conversation. And the lesson is this:

All of us need to be wanted and needed. It's important for us as humans to feel that we have some worth, something to contribute, some meaning to others, especially those we love. Mother was losing a great deal, and she very much needed to be needed.

As I realized this about Mama, it reminded me of another, similar encounter years ago with Gram when she was 99 years old and very frail. It was just a few months before she died. She was living with Mama and Dad fulltime at this point, and I was visiting prior to a meeting of the General Assembly of the Presbyterian Church. I had mimeographed a three page article on older adults that a group of us were presenting, and it needed to be collated. One evening, I mentioned to Gram that I might need her help collating this the next day. Gram, who by this time slept until past 10 am, was up soon after sunrise the next morning. She came into my bedroom and woke me up with the question: "Do you want me to help you with your project?"

As we talked with Mama over the coming days, she became increasingly interested in and committed to going to spend part of the winter with Tom and Ann. Spending the winter with family was an old tradition of ours, as Gram had spent winters with us for most of my childhood and young adult years. We began to plan for this trip of Mother's. Mother participated actively and willingly from the time that we told her that Tom and Ann needed her there with them.

For the first time in months, or years, we began to have hope that we would be able to manage her care, and finally know that we would be able to keep her healthy and safe.

As we talked, we further developed the plan. We knew that Mother would really not be able to return to Winston. It would be too dangerous. This "trip," in reality, was a move. We would be moving Mama from the place where she had lived for thirty years.

Ann had been looking at possible houses to purchase for some time, and, as we moved forward we realized this was the wisest course of action. At that time, Mother's Alzheimer's was such that she was becoming impaired and not able to live alone without help, but not so impaired that she needed to be in a caregiving situation all day. And, given our relationship and lifestyle differences, we all knew that Mother would drive Ann and Tom crazy if she lived with them. And Tom and Ann would drive her to distraction.

So Ann, the enterprising real estate agent, had already found a number of options. Luckily, she was able to locate a house with a layout much like Mama's a few blocks away from where they lived, that wasn't terribly expensive.

Luck, grace. It was a gift in any case. We arranged to buy the house for Mama and plan for her trip to Louisville.

We now had a clear plan for moving Mama.

Over time, we became engaged in spinning the yarn, and it helped. Ann managed all of the real estate tasks and the closing. The house was just a few blocks away from their home. We knew that acclimating Mother to a new *home* would be difficult at best. However, the place was very close to Tom and Ann, and had a layout that wasn't terribly different from Mama's place in Winston-Salem.

Though it didn't have the yard lot full of azaleas, we planted many that spring after we moved Mother.

We were very lucky that we had the option of buying a house near Tom and Ann. I realize that many families don't have the luxury of purchasing another property for a parent to move into and live close to one of the children. In fact, a parent's home is often sold in order to pay increasing expenses incurred in caregiving.

Increasingly, the elderly and their adult children may need to look to reverse mortgages to fund the increasing costs for caregiving. Or, they may sell property in order to move into a smaller home, a retirement community, or assisted living. They may move in with one of their children. And even though one's assets may not be what Mother's were at that time, those who are now in their seventies and eighties are often much more forward-thinking, flexible and resourceful than my Mother was.

In caregiving, each of us will find that we and our parent/s have unique needs, challenges, resources and assets. It is when we can bring our resources and assets to address our needs and challenges that we can move forward. And the answers often come as creative impulses, and ideas "out of the blue."

In our case, we had two big challenges: (1) Mother's fast declining health and memory, and (2) her absolute unwillingness to consider options and her rages and unstable behavior when she felt cornered. She had become a real risk to herself, and she was no longer able to cope alone. That was the biggest challenge. Her need was to be able to live as independently as possible with help, so that she would be protected and safe, and able to continue to enjoy her music and things she still loved.

Our resources included the three of us, her other family and friends, and our commitment to working to find good and meaningful solutions. Not every adult child has the capacity, the commitment or the dedication to do what we did. And, if you don't have that set of resources, that's all right. We do the best we can with what we have.

We are all very grateful that Mama and Dad were such savers and had the financial assets they did. Because Mama was a real mess. If we hadn't had the financial assets we had available, I cannot imagine getting through her final years.

In most cases, we can find resources and assets to address the very real and often overwhelming needs and challenges.

Do an inventory. Go to those websites and local resources that have provided help to you in the past. Look carefully at your options. Talk with people who have been through a similar situation to yours.

If your biggest challenges are finding affordable or subsidized caregiving for the work day, then look for people who have solved that problem.

If you need to find inexpensive ways to remodel a part of your house to add a bathroom to the room where you plan to move your Mother, then find people who have done something similar. Again, the local Alzheimer's Association and your local Senior Center can often provide you with invaluable free information and counsel. They can often put you in touch with much needed resources.

Anne Hays Egan

Chapter 10: Taking Care of Ourselves - Mindfulness and Self Care

Taking care of Mama was a real challenge. It was hard to know what to do. And even though I have a background in social work and health care consulting, it was still so hard. That's the way it is when you're dealing with a family member who is struggling with their own frailty and in need of a lot of support. When Alzheimer's is an issue, it simply complicates everything. She didn't realize that she was not able to care for herself when that time came.

To say that it was stressful for all of us is an understatement. Ann and Tom provided day-to-day care and managed her care for almost two years. When it was time to move Mama again from Louisville, KY to Buffalo, WY the two of them were exhausted. Absolutely wrung out.

John was then the primary caregiver for another two years, and he managed the four part-time caregivers who were there every week, as well as the woman who came to give her baths. It was exhausting and took a great deal out of John.

And we were lucky. We had family members willing to spend time with Mama, and work to manage her care. And we had some financial resources that allowed us to hire people to share the burden. Without those resources, I cannot imagine how we would have managed.

It was a burden we willingly shouldered. We loved Mama and wanted to make sure that she received the same kind of care at home that she had given her Mother. But make no mistake, the caregiving was a burden. A burden that fell primarily upon Tom, Ann and John.

We thought that we went into these decisions with our "eyes wide open." And, for the most part we did. My brothers and I are all three researchers, and that skill was invaluable to us. We researched so many aspects of Alzheimer's, different care options available, and what to expect. But, even as well-equipped as we were, there were so many surprises. The journey itself was stressful, exhausting, beautiful and sacred. All of those things.

We saw our Mother diminish over time. She grew smaller and thinner over the final years of her life, until she was quite thin and frail.

Mama's mind became foggy, and she leaned on her social skills. Then, as Alzheimer's took over her brain like the Alabama kudzu covers the hillside, we saw her continually stumble to express herself. And her efforts at socializing at the end were painful to watch.

Music was Mother's dear friend throughout the entire ordeal, and it gave her joy and pleasure and filled her life with meaning long after her mental faculties had become seriously compromised.

Her spirit was strong for most of that journey. She was usually headstrong, often controlling and very strong willed. It made caregiving sometimes difficult. And it also enabled her to soldier on with greater strength and dignity than had she caved in or given up at an earlier stage, or had a different personality type.

To see all of that in its very real presence was difficult. It was extremely stressful for all of us. There were enough times when I veged out in front of the TV with my favorite chocolate. Or ate too much. There were times I disappeared into work, and worked addictively. Any of those responses and others like drinking or gambling are all unhealthy ways we blow off steam. I exercised many of the unhealthy options, as most of us do from time to time.

But, what really gave me life, and what really helped me were the healthy stress reducers.

What are some of the healthy stress reducers that worked for me?

Since the late 1990s, I have been practicing Vipassana Buddhist mindfulness practice and meditation. That has been a godsend. I tried to meditate some every day, even if it was for a few minutes. I would sit and try to clear my mind. We have a number of meditating communities in Santa Fe, and I took advantage of group meditation as well. Today, we have even more resources that I had in the late 1990s, including wonderful meditation tapes you can play or download from YouTube, books, communities. What meditation did for me was to still my racing mind, and to help me realize that life is impermanent, and that the joys and sorrow are temporary. It provided some distance and perspective and calmed me. I'm a rather fast-paced Gemini, so calming me was a really good thing, for me and those around me!

Prayer is a wonderful practice which feeds the heart and soul. I prayed a lot. Those "Oh God, if you just do this one thing" kind of foxhole prayers, as well as regular prayers that Mother and all of us be supported and led in what we were to do. I asked friends to pray for us. I have always believed in prayer, it's just not a straight-line I-ask-God-gives kind of deal, but more like particle field theory. We share our prayers and they go into this great cosmic field. That's what I believe anyway. It was fascinating to discover that Harvard researchers were able to scientifically document the efficacy of prayer. It helped knowing that we were praying and that people were praying for us. How prayers are answered, that's for God to know, I certainly can't figure it out.

As we continued providing care for Mama, we began to encourage one another to take time off, and to take time out. We encouraged each other to look at little opportunities to relax and rejuvenate.

And, I recommend that to anyone who is a caregiver for an elderly parent. Look for ways to feed your mind, your body, your spirit and your soul. What each of us needs is particular to us as an individual. One person's tonic is another one's toxin. But, when we give ourselves healthy little gifts throughout the weeks and months, it makes the journey so much easier.

"It is a marathon and not a sprint." Gloria Steinem said that about the feminist movement back in the 1970s, and it applies as well to caregiving. Pace yourself. Try to realize early on that you won't get everything right. You won't get a lot of things right. However, if you get the big things right, you're doing wonderfully. Wonderfully, indeed.

Each of us has our own unique personality, skills and needs. Take an inventory of yourself, and that will help you determine what might best help you to reduce stress:

1. What can you give, and how do you want to provide help?

2. What do you find difficult to do, that you'd like for someone else to handle? Perhaps another family member, friend or neighbor can handle some of those things. Or some may have to go by the wayside.

3. What do you need to recharge your batteries? What gives you food for your soul. It could be a walk outside, or spending time with a grandchild, or some special project that nurtures you. Find ways to take blocks of time to feed your soul – an afternoon, or a day. Whatever you can manage. Then, find little tiny slices of time where you can nurture yourself. A fifteen minute stroll over your lunch

break, or a quiet moment in prayer. It's whatever fits for you.

Self-care is so important for all caregivers. We often find that we become sick as a result of caregiving, and it can certainly age us. Mother had taken care of Dad during his final years battling cancer. After he died, we realized she had aged a great deal, and she became ill.

So, take care of yourself. Look at ways that you can reduce your stress. Nurture yourself. Take time for yourself. Even when it feels like you don't have a minute to spare, do things that feed your spirit.

Chapter 11: Packing and the Farewell Party

Once we had our plans for moving Mama, things moved along well. Thank goodness! It had been a very stressful few years, for the most part. So it was always nice to come upon an easy patch. Friends of hers came forward, and we planned a number of parties for her.

We had a bit of experience with the party business. The year before, we had held a retirement party for Mama. It had been clear then that she was no longer able to manage her three remaining music students, and we felt she needed some help to retire. We didn't want her to find that her last few students petered away, with no recognition of her work and her contributions.

The retirement party started out as a simple and small affair at home with current and former piano students, during what was to be her next to last Christmas in Winston-Salem. We worked with a few of the families she had taught for years to plan a party. John, the youngest, knew many of the families and worked to contact them. It was amazing how many people were interested in coming to pay their regards, and their respects.

Mama was an excellent piano teacher, focusing on the unique talents, needs and issues of each student. She would spend hours at the music store poring over pieces she thought each student would find challenging and interesting. No student was ever turned away for lack of funds, and she provided scholarships where needed.

About 25 or 30 people showed up for an afternoon where we feted Mama. She loved it. A few of her former students made presentations and comments. Many brought food. We had a silver tray engraved, and provided her with that along with a host of other "goodies."

It was a wonderful event that surpassed our expectations. She had given a lot to the community, and people were happy to share their thanks and best wishes.

We wanted something like that for her as we planned to move her. We worked with her friends at the church to schedule a party for her after church the Sunday after Christmas. Her friends knew that this was a good-bye, but we billed it as a "Farewell for the Winter."

This provided her and her friends with the opportunity to say "good-bye." Closure is important for all of us, and we wanted this to be possible for her and her friends, even with the challenges that accompanied her departure.

The party was a lovely affair, with many people dropping by to wish her well. As usual, Mama was somehow able to be "up" for the event. Even with what was now moderate Alzheimer's, she rose to the occasion. She greeted people and talked with everyone.

It was amazing to see how well her deeply ingrained Southern social skills helped her. When in doubt, she could fall back upon:

"Oh, it's so nice to see you again."
"Yes, I'm looking forward to this trip."
"Thanks so much for coming."

These social skills were so deeply ingrained, they were part of her old memory that lasted long into her dementia. They were second nature to her. And they served her very, very well.

People were genuinely sad to see her go. She had been an active volunteer in the Presbyterian Church and a strong supporter. Years before, she was the President of Presbyterian Women. She had quite a few friends from those years, as well as others she had met more recently, like Louise. The room was full, and it filled her and us.

When a parent is struggling with Alzheimer's, we all suffer through a series of small losses. It's a terrible thing to have people, places and things just fade away. We all need the opportunity to grieve these losses and to have closure whenever possible.

I remember when I was serving as a chaplain at Riverview Home for the Aged in Philadelphia. There was a wonderful old man there named Bobby who people loved because he was self-effacing, and funny. And he was a man in a sea of women. He died. And his death almost went by without notice. Except that people told me about it, and we put together a ceremony. Some shuffled in. Some were attentive, and others were in a fog. But they told him they loved him. The respected his memory. It brought them peace.

Take note of these times if you can, as you go through your own journey with your parent, your partner or other loved one. Take a few moments to acknowledge these changes in ways that fit for your own family It's a way of honoring them and yourselves.

Chapter 12: Driving Down to Georgia

We left not on "The Midnight Train to Georgia," but in my rental car following the church farewell party for Mama. She was on a high as we left the church, and so pleased that people had come out to wish her well as she went to Louisville "for the winter." But like Gladys, we, too had a one way ticket, and Mama was not to return to Winston-Salem. From the church parking lot, we headed out of town and Southward. I had packed Mama's suitcases and mine the day before and my rental car was loaded and ready for the trip.

For a while, Mama didn't notice we were driving on the interstate, away from Winston. However, after we had chatted about the party for over a half hour, she finally commented:
"When will we get home?"
And then, "This doesn't look familiar. Are we going the right way?"

Even with Alzheimer's, she had moments when she was quite sharp. And, they would almost invariably come at the worst possible time.

After thinking for a few minutes, I came up with some of the excuses I had worked on for the previous few days.
"Mama, we're headed down to Tula's. The weather is getting bad, and a snowstorm is heading our way. We had to leave from church to miss it."
"But I haven't changed. And, I haven't even packed."

She started to fidget, and I began to worry. She had opened a car door when the car was moving once or twice before, and I dreaded the prospect of her doing that on I-40.

"Mama, we packed yesterday, do you remember? And I have your suitcase in the trunk. We're all set."

She turned and looked at me with a withering glance, not all that unknown to me. I chatted away. Finally, we either found a radio station that played the Andrews Sisters, or I started singing "Chattanooga Choo Choo." After a while, we were both singing through our now limited repertoire of WWII songs.

After that, I finally relaxed. The drive down to Athens, Georgia was only about 5 or 6 hours, and a nice, easy trip most of the time. My nerves dragged it out, I'm sure. But, after the musical interlude, we chatted away, commenting on the landscape, music and the upcoming visit with Tula.

Mother was looking forward to the visit once her concerns had been addressed. Tula was the second youngest sibling, six years her senior, and they had always been very close. In fact, when Gram had been absorbed in art projects and music lessons, it was Tula who had made sure that Mama had a good breakfast and was dressed properly for school, and the one who made sure that her homework was finished, and school requirements met. Mama sometimes called Tula her "Little Mama" when she was growing up.

Soon after dark, we arrived in Athens, tired, hungry and ready for a break. Tula was, as always, welcoming and happy to see us. But, she was showing a new level of tension. After Mother had gone to bed, Tula mentioned to me that, although she felt that we were doing the right thing for Mother, she was still a bit upset. And, she shared that it was hard for her to see her little sister struggling with dementia. In fact, Tula was much sharper than Mama, and it was disconcerting for her most of all.

We visited Tula for a week .I realized later that our visit had been extremely draining for Tula. It was heartbreaking for her to see her little sister confused, rather often inarticulate, sometimes glassy-eyed, and clearly in the grip of a mental monster.

Mother had begun to have what people often call "the Alzheimer's look." When she was tired or confused, her eyes would glass over, a vapid smile would take over her mouth, and she would appear almost childlike. Her face was beginning to change. Her vocabulary was diminishing markedly. And Mother, who always paid a great deal of attention to her appearance, started to look rumpled and unkempt.

The difference between Mother and Tula was significant. Tula and I would both manage our conversation so that the topics were familiar to Mama, and the language simplified in order to keep her engaged. But engagement was becoming more of a challenge.

The visit was pleasant, however. Tula was incredibly helpful. More than helpful, she was absolutely key to our being able to handle the change. We did things that were fun. And music, which was always a bond between all three of us, continued to serve.

It was amazing to see how much more ably Mother behaved when either talking about music or playing the piano. Many who are experts in the field of dementia have found that those who play musical instruments and who have spent their lives steeped in music tend to not forget music in the same way they forget recent events during early and mid-stages of Alzheimer's disease.

One of the most important things you can do when helping a loved one with Alzheimer's is to provide opportunities for them to listen to their favorite music, to sing songs they love. If they play a musical instrument, it's important for them to try to keep a hand in, playing what they can. Music enlivens people and helps them connect with life.

Chapter 13: Difficult Family Relationships

It took me until I was well into my thirties before I realized that Mama, who we had always called "a little bit crazy," was, in reality mentally ill. Southern women were often given latitude to be a bit bonkers, as part of one's creativity and personal drama. And, Southern family stories and literature are full of tales of women who were much more interesting because of the drama created around them. Mama certainly brought drama into our lives.

She was brilliant, beautiful, creative, and a marvelous teacher. She provided us with a wonderful education. She ensured that our young lives were filled with learning, culture, adventure, and travel. And she often lived on the edge.

Initially, it was hard to admit that my Mother was crazy, or mentally ill. The realization dawned gradually, as I worked on my own issues and accustomed myself to that reality. By my late thirties, I had done a lot of inner work with the help of therapists, and finally began to see through the swaddling of denial I had been wrapped in for so long.

Mama had given me many wonderful things. These gifts she provided were quite substantial and included a love for music and the arts, a wonderful education (including graduate school), culture and travel. But she also provided me with the very difficult legacy of her mental illness, perhaps equivalent in import to her positive legacy. The twin drivers of her inner demons and the force of her personality when facing challenges were for many years, rather overwhelming.

Like other adult children, my brothers and I tried to ferret out the cause of Mother's craziness, and had many discussions about the issue. Her Father, a brilliant doctor who graduated from Vanderbilt Medical School at age 23, had lost very few patients and had helped to build one of the great hospitals in Birmingham.

According to family legend, he initially drank when he would lose a patient. But, eventually, he probably drank to drink. His brilliance came with an extremely volatile personality and a temper that became infamous. Gram was as calm and unperturbed as Grandfather was temperamental. We often said that Mother took after her Father, and that her older sister Tula took after Gram.

So, we believed that at least some of Mother's emotional instability came from her genetic predisposition, or nature. A lot may have come from her life experiences, or nurture.

I learned after I was grown that Gram had always kept a suitcase packed for herself and Mama, when Mother was a child. As his alcoholism progressed, Grandfather would increasingly fly into rages. Sometimes, He would break the furniture, Gram would quickly shepherd the children out of the house and to a friend's or to the Y.

The stress this must have created is hard to imagine. Harder still to imagine would be Mother's ambivalence about her Father. When she was five years old, she suffered a burst appendix. He performed an emergency appendectomy and saved her life. In the early 1920s, few children lived through a ruptured appendix. So the Father who created chaos and havoc in her later childhood was the same Father who had saved her life in what was a celebrated surgical success.

Even though Mother glamorized her experiences in World War II, and in many ways saw them as the highlight of her life, the war must have been extremely frightening and stressful. Her experience was much more than the series of parties, musicals and skits for the enlisted men, dates with officers, and exciting travel.

As part of historical research for a thesis, my brother John discovered that many of the Red Cross women helped GIs write their last letters home. They were part of the terrible medical triage that occurred after battle, ministering to those who were placed in the "too sick to survive" and the "very ill and waiting for surgery or treatment" categories. Mother also saw the crew of the Enola Gay take off and return, after the atomic bombing run to Hiroshima. Her only comment was that the crew returned "shell shocked," and that they were "quickly escorted away for debriefing."

After she married, she and the family moved with Dad every few years with each new Red Cross assignment. Although she tried to make the best of things by building music and travel into our experiences, the frequent moves must have been stressful for her. In retrospect, I realize that, in spite of the wonderful cultural experiences this travel afforded, it provided little stability or a home anchor. Gram was the anchor – for all of us.

The moves continued, and we relocated to Puerto Rico in 1963 from Montgomery, Alabama. For me, the multi-racial environment was a lifesaver. But, Puerto Rico was more difficult for Mother, because her support network was removed. She suffered greater stress, and her behavior became more erratic. Even though she had what she called "knock-down-drag-out-fights" before we moved to Puerto Rico, the episodes increased after our move. Mother would frequently fly into rages, scream and lash out at me or my brothers.

At this point, Mother began a long descent into episodes of mental illness punctuated by periods of brilliance and strong engagement with the community. As a young teen-ager, I found a number of escapes, mostly productive. These included excelling at school, scheduling after-school activities, music and baby-sitting whenever I had the opportunity. The combination of these allowed me to limit my time at home, but not enough. Mother began to have violent episodes that often (but not always) came on her like a bad thunderstorm. We could usually first see or sense the clouds, and then the clouds darkening as her spirit became increasingly agitated and "looking for a fight."

During the rest of my teen years, and my younger brothers' teen years, Mother continued to have these rages and fights. She was often able to maintain a public face of Southern charm and professionalism as she taught school and volunteered in the community. The term 'child abuse' was not yet the common parlance we find today, and people did not interfere. I did have a number of adult neighbors who had me babysit for them, and who more or less "adopted" me, and encouraged me to spend time with them in their homes. I've often wondered how much the neighbors heard. When Mother was in one of her episodes, she would scream at the top of her lungs, as would we. Sometimes she would run outside screaming, too. It was probably not a secret. But nobody I knew mentioned that they understood the hell we all lived with. And nobody suggested that she might need help.

Like so many families with problems and secrets, we all suffered. Our relationships were a strange amalgam of care and great opportunities mixed with threats and violence. We learned at young ages to check the temperature of the house whenever we came home. We became hyper-vigilant. We also internalized the message that we, as the children, were to blame for the family's arguments and difficulties.

Whenever Mother had one of her rages, she would take to her bed, with a "spell." Dad's role was then to minister to her, and care for her as she dealt with migraines. Before we could go to bed on any such day, he would round us up and force us to apologize to our now prostrate and very ill Mother for having made her sick. Each of us would apologize in our own way, and then she would tell us that she loved us, and that tomorrow would be a better day. And each of us carried this internalized self blaming with us into adulthood.

Decades later, when Mother began to show signs of dementia, it took all three of us working together to find a way to deal with her. We had never gained full adult or emancipated status in Mother's eyes, even as middle-aged adults. So taking charge took effort, coordination, "moxie," - and therapy. In a strange twist of fate, it was Mother's model of caring for her own Mother, Gram, at home that gave us some of our guidance.

Some might wonder why we didn't report the abuse, or run away, or distance ourselves further once we were adults. It was what it was.

John and I did a lot of our own work, to make peace with our childhoods, and to gain a firmer footing as adults. As children, we knew our family was troubled, but we didn't realize that we were that unusual. There were few venues in the 1950s and 1960s for lodging complaints or getting help for oneself and one's parents. I knew I fought with my Mother more than did my friends, but I didn't dare talk about all that happened at home. "Nice families" just didn't do that.

Gram took care of me every summer, when I would usually stay with her long after the rest of the family left to go back home. She also came to live with us in the winter. She was my favorite person in the world, and my lifeline.

My parents put me through college and graduate school. By the time I realized that something had been very wrong with at least part of my childhood, I was working on my own issues. I also realized that my parents had done quite well with their investments. They helped me a number of times during my twenties and thirties, and then later on began gifting each of us annually to reduce the size of their estate.

As an adult, I did not want to rock the boat and jeopardize their financial assistance and my inheritance. I felt that they owed me. The problem with that attitude was that it kept me angry, dependent and financially dysfunctional for many years of my adult life.

Now, as someone in her sixties and looking back at the decades, I am amazed that three of us have done as well as we have. All of us have graduate degrees: Tom with his Ph.D.; John with an A.B.D. Ph.D. (All But Dissertation), and me with an M.Div. and an A.B.D. We've all contributed to our communities and feel good about what we've done with our lives. And, I believe that each of us has made peace with Mother and our childhoods. She had significant handicaps, and she did the best she could with those. Today, we're all a bit more sanguine about those experiences. We appreciate what she gave us; we are saddened by the damage she inflicted. And we've moved on with our lives.

If you have issues with your loved one who has dementia (and most of us have), deal with them if at all possible. Work through those issues with a therapist. Support and self-help groups can also be helpful. I didn't have regrets when Mother died, and I'm very grateful for that. Whenever possible, take care of those issues so that you can make peace with them and yourself. Making peace doesn't necessarily mean "making nice." Part of making peace for me before Mother became ill meant setting boundaries with her, and limiting time spent during visits to reduce the potential for arguments. Dealing with my issues and making peace allowed me to accept her more easily during her final years, and to have no regrets when she died.

Anne Hays Egan

Picture Gallery

Mother and me in 1952, taking a break on a trip through the Smoky Mountains.

Dad and me in 1955, in front of our house in Chamblais, France. This chateau was bombed during WW II and still had a few holes in the roof. The pipes froze during the record-breaking cold in the winter of 1955-1956. I went to a one room schoolhouse nearby (no kidding).

Mama came from a family of educators. Gram taught piano and art. Both aunts were teachers; Sister taught piano and Tula taught violin. Uncle Bill was a school superintendent. Mama taught piano.

My two brothers and me (John's in the middle), dressed in Confederate Drag as part of Montgomery's Centennial Celebration in 1961. It was such a big deal one would think the South had won that war. It was over 40 years later when Mother died that we discovered that Great Grandfather Asa B. Hays and his best friend, Jack Curtis, had left the Confederacy for the Union Army. Big, big family secret.

Mama standing near one of the fortress corners at Ft. Brooke, in the early
1970s. Ft. Brooke, or La Fortaleza, is one of the historic landmarks in
San Juan, Puerto Rico. It dates to the early conquistadors, complete with
Casa Blanca, the Governor's Palace, and underground tunnels to the sea.
Our move from Montgomery to San Juan in 1963 was a positive multi-
cultural, life-changing experience for me.

Mother and Dad in 1989 in Harper's Ferry, VA. Dad had been sick with
cancer for a number of years. He and Mother travelled a great deal
during those last years before he died in 1992.

Chapter 14: Getting Adjusted to Louisville and Selling the Winston House

Once Mama was settling into the new place in Louisville, we started to talk about how to handle the now empty house in Winston-Salem. We knew we wanted to sell it, but didn't want to just sell it out from under her. She would surprise us from time to time and talk about Winston and the house. We usually found a way to change the subject.

We were concerned about the empty house, and the potential for problems with upkeep or any emergency. It was now spring, and we also realized that the best time to sell the house would be during the spring or summer. We began to look for a realtor in Winston, discuss the sale, look at any work that needed to be done, and pricing the house.

It is always a challenge to handle a house sale long distance, which is what most of us face was we care for elderly parents. Having a knowledgeable resource like Ann was a big help. She guided us in finding a realtor who had a high success rate, was knowledgeable, trustworthy and a good fit. When we sell a house long distance, we depend heavily on the realtor in our parent's home town, and having a good relationship is extremely important.

So, my brother John came up with an idca to help Mama divest herself of the house – emotionally and actually.

He and Tom talked with Mother about the house in Winston needing a number of repairs, especially to the old clay pipes that were under the large front lawn. There had been some damage to the pipes. In recent years, roots of the old trees had been seeking water, and found and entered the pipes, making them run slowly.

John and Tom simply accelerated the issue, and prepared a summary of high possible costs for upkeep.

Mama looked at the list and tossed it down on the table in disgust.

"Why don't we just sell the damn house," she said.

And so we did.

Helping a parent sell a house from a distance is a challenge at best. And, each family has its own dynamics that can either help you move forward with whatever decision is most appropriate and those that impede progress. Work carefully, and make sure that you have excellent real estate resources.

Chapter 15: When They Forget Who You Are

Mother's much loved sister and my aunt Tula died in the late 1990s. The family was planning her Memorial Service for a month or two after her death. My two brothers and I agreed that we should wait to tell Mother in person, when one of us could be with her. I was planning to visit a few weeks later, so the task was delegated to me.

When I thought it was a good time to talk, I told Mama about Tula's illness and death. She took it hard, but stoically, as I thought she might. Although she didn't dwell on her death, she did remember later on that Tula had passed away. Since she had lost a lot of her short term memory by then, it was a tribute to her relationship with her older much loved sister that she remembered it at all.

My brothers and I discussed the Memorial Service with our cousins. Since Tula had been a violinist and music teacher, the family planned a lot of music for the service, including a string quartet. We thought that having music would be an appropriate tribute to Tula. It would make the service easier and more meaningful for the family, and would certainly be something Mother could appreciate.

Tom and Ann started talking with Mother about the service, asking her if she wanted to go. In her more lucid moments, she was quite clear about wanting to go with Tom and my sister-in-law to the service. My brother, John and I each flew into Atlanta and drove over to Athens. Tom and Ann, drove down from Louisville with Mother. We all met at our Cousin Jenny's house outside of Atlanta. Ever the wonderful hostess, Jenny had prepared a wonderful spread of cold cuts and salads for us. It was a great gathering, as some of us hadn't seen each other for quite a few years.

I could tell that Mother was exhausted, but my brother and sister-in-law were absolutely wiped out. They explained that the ride down had been quite difficult. Mama had been agitated and fretful, and she fussed throughout the drive down from Louisville. They were never sure if Mother was going to suddenly open a car door while the car was going 75 miles an hour.

She was not having a good day, which meant that nobody else was having a good day either.

Once at Jenny's house, though, Mama perked up. She always had the ability to "put on her best face," to be charming, especially in social settings. Even with her Alzheimer's, she could still socialize and fall back upon manners and social skills she had honed for decades. It really was fascinating to watch.

After eating, I got up to check on something in the next room. As I came back into the dining room, I saw Mother standing quite still and watching me with her head tilted and a quizzical expression on her face.

When she saw me return, she began to walk toward me looking confused. Then she said, "You look so familiar." All conversation ceased, time stopped, and the room was totally silent. For our family, that was highly unusual.

Even though we had talked about the fact that Mother would forget who we were, we thought we were prepared; we weren't. At least, we weren't emotionally prepared. I wasn't prepared for that bombshell.

I don't know where my answer came from, it just came.
"That's because you've known me all my life," I said and gave her
a hug.

She hugged me back and gave me a big smile, and saying, "Oh,
yes," confusion momentarily relieved. I felt like throwing up.

It turned out that the afternoon at Jenny's was one of Mother's
high points during the trip for Tula's Memorial Service - - that and
the service itself. We were to stay at Tula's house, since it was
familiar to Mother. And once there, it was strange. We were
surrounded by Tula's spirit and her things – and she wasn't there.

Mama was restless and at odds with us and herself, so we tried to
keep everything as simple as possible, fix dinner and get her to go
to bed. We hoped that tomorrow would be a better day. I was in the
middle of reading **Divine Secrets of the Ya Ya Sisterhood**, and
stayed up late, immersed in the intertwined stories of my past and
hers.

Early the next morning, we got up and had breakfast. Mama was
not doing well. She was confused and full of questions. Finally, we
adjourned to get dressed. My sister-in-law, Ann came into my
room a few minutes later.

"Anne, Mama needs your help. She won't let me help her get
dressed. She's taken my bra, put it on over her PJs, and says she's
now ready to go to church." "Oh, brother," I muttered and
followed Ann down the hall.

Sure enough, Mama was sitting on the bed, looking pleased with
herself for getting dressed by herself. She had on the bra over her
pajamas. A good two or three sizes too large, the bra was

hilariously telegraphing her arrival. I tried a number of tactics, and she was just not willing to budge. Finally, I came upon some solution I can't remember now. We got her dressed. Ann recovered her bra and got dressed. And, in a short while, we met the rest of the family for lunch. Afterward, we went over to the church.

First Presbyterian in Athens is a beautiful, quintessentially mainline Protestant church (minus the tall white steeple). It has a beautiful Georgian styled brick exterior and an open, sunny sanctuary. I had been many times when visiting Tula and my cousins, and always enjoyed it as much for the aesthetics as for the services. Mama was a bit shaky but on her best behavior. She somehow knew that the service was for her sister who had died, and she was quiet and respectful. The music was beautiful, and the string quartet was a tribute to Tula and her life in music. Afterward, we took a family photo, and when I looked at it later, I could see the continuing ravages of Alzheimer's on Mama's face.

We went by Tula's house for the last time. Everyone visited, though briefly. We all needed to travel home, and it had been a long day.

One of the moments we fear the most is when a parent forgets who we are. It is a dreaded event. We may worry about it, wonder when it will happen, or hope that it won't happen. It usually does happen at some point. With Mama, she realized that we were all family throughout her illness, but she didn't really understand that we were her children, at least part of the time. There's nothing that will prepare you for the shock. It's one of the many little "good-byes" that we face when we are caring for a loved one with Alzheimer's. Talk with others about it. Get some support. And try to realize that it is not about you. It's the disease. And, it's one of the saddest parts of dementia.

Chapter 16: Tough Choices and Taking Charge

Mama could not function without a lot of help, and we now were handling all of her care, financial affairs, and the house sale. Everything. But, she still had enough moments of lucidity that she would often argue with us about how things needed to be done.

After all, she was the Mother and we were her children. She had a deep need to be in charge. And she would stubbornly assert her will at the most interesting times.

She did not like to go to the doctor, and, when Mama was living in Louisville, it took all of Ann's persuasive skills to get her dressed, out the door and to the doctor's office. One time, Dr. H. was running late. Very late. After about 20 to 30 minutes of waiting, Mama announced: "This is ridiculous. I'm going home."

She promptly stood up and stormed out. Ann ran to catch up with her. Mama was moving fast, and seemed to know her way out of the building and to the parking lot. Ann took her home, and they had to reschedule.

It wasn't easy to take charge of situations with a Mother who had such a tight hold on things. But we had to do it. Sometimes gradually, when that was possible. However, Mama was losing her ability to care for herself, so there were many times when one of her children or a caregiver had to "lay down the law," as she would say.

Thank goodness, she didn't try to drive anymore. And, she didn't leave the house and wander, as some people do. But, she tried to turn on the stove from time to time. And, she would do interesting things with appliances.

We would often post large signs. We had to remove some of the appliances.

And, there were times when we had to take charge and order her to do something. Like get dressed. Or brush her teeth. Or get in the car to go somewhere, like the doctor's office.

She couldn't dress herself any more without help from someone else, but she didn't want the help and often complained. So we shopped for dresses for her that were easy to pull on and take off. We had to reduce the number of buttons or snaps or other "do-Dads" as she called them. They were confusing, and made dressing more complicated and difficult for us all. Someone who had been a fashion plate all of her life had taken to dresses that were shapeless and simple. Thank God she no longer paid much attention to her appearance, or cared. And she seldom looked into the mirror anymore, whether from lack of interest or lack of will, we never knew. Everything became scaled down and simplified.

We didn't realize that she wasn't brushing her teeth anymore right away. It's one of those personal grooming habits that, for good reason, remains personal. However, at one visit I noticed that her teeth were a mess. I tried to get her to brush them with very mixed results. We never knew if she had forgotten how to brush her teeth, or didn't want to bother, or found some element of the exercise confusing or frightening. During my visits, I could occasionally get her to brush, sometimes as I was brushing my teeth. But we ended up pretty much accepting that it would be hit or miss. That was one of the things that we let slide.

She seemed to be taking care of bathing occasionally and going to the toilet by herself. Her skills there were starting to slip as well, but not as badly. That was something we knew we would need to address in the future.

Sometimes Mama would defer and do what we asked. More often, she would argue. Or stomp out. Or sometimes she would cry and become hysterical. We tried to find creative ways to get her to do things. Subterfuge became a fine art form.

As the dementia progressed, she became more mellow and a bit more pliable. She would do things we asked more easily oftentimes. Or, she would more willingly participate in activities like eating or getting dressed.

It was a mixed blessing.

Taking charge was hard for us. I think it's hard for most adult children. The roles are reversed, and until we have some practice with being the parent to our parent, it's uncomfortable. In our case, uncomfortable was an understatement. It was just tough.

Personal care is one of those items I'd never talked much to anyone about after I was 10 years old or so. It was one's personal business. I would notice when someone was disheveled, or dirty, or poorly put together. Seldom did I hear much discussion about personal care except in the most summary and rather clinical fashion when older adult serving agencies would describe their services.

"We provide caregiving, which includes offering companionship, assistance with tasks around the house, personal care, and support."

That sounds rather innocuous. But, those of us who have now provided personal care to a frail elderly person know that it is confusing, complicated and difficult for the adult child as well as the parent. If you're able to read about this, or talk with professional caregivers, that might provide you with a great deal of help.

Over the last few years of Mother's life, we consulted with her caregivers for their advice about how to handle these caregiving tasks. However, probably not enough. We researched many areas related to Mama's care, but not much in this area.

Some of our values, attitudes and habits are ingrained early on. We learned from Mama and Gram not to talk about personal care issues, hygiene, the body, the toilet, sex or anything else related to those topics. My Grandother was born in 1882 and had Victorian and Edwardian values and extremely conservative habits. So, those were passed down through the generations, from Gram to her daughters, and from Mama to me. It's not discussed. That's that. Most people now are not that rigid, which is a blessing.

However, no matter what your family culture and traditions, one often finds that it is difficult and embarrassing to be in the position of dressing or undressing one's Mother, or giving her a bath, or helping her to go to the toilet.

We learned from our caregivers to try to keep things as simple as possible. We realized that it helped to keep things calm, respectful, and matter of fact. Be gentle and patient, remembering that all of us will be in that same situation someday. Some people find that having caregivers handle these personal care tasks is one of the most helpful things they can do. And, if that's your situation, I would encourage you to get all the support you can in that area.

If you find that you need to handle many of these tasks yourself, talk with others who have helped a parent or loved one. Talk with professional caregivers. And look on national caregiving websites to find out recommended ways to handle personal care.

Anne Hays Egan

Chapter 17: Stories and Playacting

Southerners love stories, as I've said a number of times in this book. I always realized that story was a big part of my history and culture. But it wasn't until I started working on this book that I realized that story is deeply rooted in me, and in Mama's side of the family.

Gram used to tell stories about what it was like to grow up in the late 1880s, before the turn of the last century. She'd talk about taking the train from home to Athens, where she went to school and college. She would write home for hair ribbons and art supplies. Her husband-to-be met her during her senior year, and he "came courting." She would laugh as she talked about her aborted attempts to learn to drive. Dr. Whorton had a Model T Ford, and she lost control of it, running down a little hill and tipping over the car. As she emerged, she informed her husband that he would simply have to drive her everywhere or she would take the streetcar. And, that's what she did for her entire life.

Gram's memories of her long history were shared with us through years of family stories. She told tales about growing up in north Alabama, and her Father, the Judge, who admonished her to not eat so many sweets. She talked about the early days when Dr. Whorton was developing his practice, and about her art exhibitions. She would often share the stories behind her paintings of Jefferson Davis, Stonewall Jackson, and Speaker Bankhead – as well as her paintings of each of her children. She would talk about how she and Aunt Blanche (her best friend for 70 years) would get in trouble in school, and how they helped each other as young Mothers with their children. Stories were a central part of growing up under her tutelage.

When we were children we spent part of each summer at Gram's.
After dinner, the grownups would all go into the living room to
visit. Most summers, we had Sister (who lived up the hill), and
Tula – and their kids. And, Uncle Bill would often come up from
South Alabama, where he and his family lived. Once the adults
were in the living room catching up, we children would shut the
dining room door, pull the tablecloth back down, and get under the
table (now a tent) to hear Jenny's newest ghost stories. She would
keep us spellbound for hours, making them up as she went along.
Our cousin Palmer was her sidekick, and made the sound effects. I
can still remember some of the gorier stories, and the scraping
sound of the old blind boatman, with the flickering light of the boat
as it made its way with its human cargo down some hidden
underground culvert.

My cousin Margaret also shared stories of a very different kind.
She was much older, and almost grown by the time I was old
enough to read. Margaret had a stash of comic books and Mad
Magazines that were the envy of all of the cousins. When Gram
had a houseful of family, it was only the older cousins who had the
privilege of going back up the hill with Sister at the end of the
evening to spend the night with her and Margaret, and the comic
books. I was one of the lucky ones, along with Jenny and Carolyn.
My brothers stayed down at Gram's. Sister shared stories and junk
food, both of which we loved.

Mama and Gram often told the story about how Mama contracted
appendicitis when she was about 5 years old, which is mentioned
earlier in this book. They told stories about growing up with a
doctor in the family, with some of the tales actually memorialized
in the history of Norwood/Carraway Hospital in Birmingham.
They didn't tell the other stories, about how Grandfather's world
was overcome with alcohol, or Grandmother's struggles during the

Depression. Those were seldom mentioned, and when shared, were often told in whispers - as if the ghosts had ears.

So it was no surprise that Mama also liked to tell stories, and could weave a story along with the best of them. Some of her favorite stories were about her experiences in Guam and Tinian during WWII. There were stories about the performances they produced for the soldiers and sailors assigned there during the war. She talked often about the other Red Cross women with whom she had shared so much, and who remained close friends from then until each passed on. She told about sleeping on one of the surrender swords; and the antics of the "Red Cross Girls." Often, her stories about Guam and Tinian sounded more like summer camp tales than WWII in the Pacific theater. However, from time to time, when she was in a serious or reflective mood, she would let us in on just a little of the pathos and the loss that were part of her life there. And, we realized as adults, that she had seen a great deal of suffering and death there and that the singing was a way to help them all get through it.

Mama told stories about her trip with Gram to New York City, when Gram went to Columbia for an art class or workshop in the early 1930s. And, the pictures of the two of them there "doing the town" are funny and whimsical. They clearly had a great time.

Mother would tell us stories about the difficult and frighteningly cold winter of 1955-1956, when she and Dad moved the family from Chamblais to Metz France in the middle of one of the worst ice storms on record. The pipes froze. It was almost impossible to drive. And it was dark and sleeting for most of the time they managed the move.

Perhaps our history of storytelling as a family helped us to move Mama and take care of her. For, as we became involved in trying to develop the best and most appropriate care for her, we found ourselves telling her stories that would help her make sense of those things that were confusing. We told stories to get her to do things – like move from Winston-Salem. And we told stories to try to get her to eat, wear adult diapers, and take baths. And, over time, we became engrossed in these stories and started to live in them, whether they were true, partially true, or total fabrications.

Chapter 18: Getting Help Around the House

Within a few months after Mother's move to Louisville, Tom and Ann realized that she needed more help at home than they could provide on a daily basis. Mama was declining rapidly, and needed help preparing meals and just getting through the day. The two of them spent hours each day in caregiving, but there were gaps that needed to be filled.

Initially, Tom talked with Mama about getting a housekeeper. Her response was, by now, predictable. She didn't want one. She didn't need one. She felt she couldn't afford one. And, she would not be convinced. They continued to push her, and she pushed back.

Even though Mama had declined, and was having more memory problems, she could still rise to the occasion, not as splendidly as before. But she could be a force and command attention, especially when it involved an intrusion into her world. She was adamant, still somewhat articulate, and extremely difficult.

Finally, either Ann or Tom must have remembered the conversations that were so effective in getting Mama to agree to come to Louisville in the first place, and they began to make headway. They talked with her about this friend of theirs who really needed Mama's help. Robbie was a young widow whose husband had died just a few years before of a brain tumor. She had been through some very tough time, and it was true that she would benefit from another part-time housekeeping/caregiving job.

So, finally, Mother relented in order to help Tom's friend, Robbie. Thank goodness.

Robbie began her work ostensibly as a housekeeper, as far as Mother was concerned. But, she was really Mama's first hired caregiver. She did take care of the house. She also cared for Mama in a wonderful way. She fixed meals and took Mama for rides. A "tough cookie," Robbie could cut through a lot of Mama's defenses, arguments and posturing, which was wonderful for all of us, especially Tom and Ann. Robbie was the first person who took absolutely no guff from our Mother.

Gradually, Mama accepted Robbie, and learned to count on her for help around the house, fixing meals, caring for the cat, going grocery shopping and to doctor's appointments, and going out for drives and ice cream. It worked well. And Mama came to love her and consider her a good friend.

We all felt like we were on our way. And we were, for a while.

Being close to one of her children allowed for much closer supervision and support. Because she was not living with Tom and Ann, the pressures were reduced somewhat. Being able to hire support made a huge difference. For the first year or so, Mama was in good shape.

Whenever John or I would visit during the first year, we would help her to plant azaleas. Mother loved her azaleas. She and Dad had planted several hundred azaleas in Winston-Salem, and she missed them. Within a short time, there were about a few dozen azaleas covering parts of the front, back and side yard.

Alzheimer's is a sneaky disease, full of shifts. There are ups and downs with the good and bad days. There are times when a parent will hit a plateau, where there aren't the usual ups, downs, changes and dramas. Things may seem more consistent. And your parent may appear to be doing rather well. This is what happened during Mama's first year in Louisville, after we hired Robbie to help with her care.

But, the plateaus often lure us into a false sense of stability. Things start to hum along without a lot of change. The ups and downs have evened out, and that is extremely comforting.

Enjoy the plateaus. They offer a chance for you as the caregiver to recuperate and enjoy time with your loved ones. The plateaus end, and a new stage begins where there are more memory losses and greater challenges.

To understand these stages, and the plateaus, read some of the books and visit elder care resource websites that are recommended at the end of this book.

Anne Hays Egan

Chapter 19: Finding Entertainment: The Magic of Music

"You know, Mother has almost stopped reading," Tom shared with me at our next visit, which was right before Christmas.
"You're kidding," was my response.
"Oh, she still has the **Daily Word** by her bed, but she isn't reading. I haven't seen her with a book in weeks, perhaps months." He looked at me and shook his head.

We were a reading family. When I was growing up, we would read all the time during our summers spent at Gram's. She had bookcases all over the house. She had the old ones with the glass doors that slide up and back in above the shelf. She had the dark old open faced tall oak shelves at the top of the stairs that had Grandfather Whorton's medical books, Mother's old McGuffey's Readers, and countless other books. And there were the small bookcases in the bedroom where I slept that had the 1882 *Cyclopedias* (precursor to the encyclopedia). She also had early turn-of-the-century editions of *National Geographic*, which I loved. Those early National Geographic Magazines and our own life in Europe provided the many virtual and real travel experiences that created my own personal set-point that has always caused me to relish travel.

When we were growing up, we all read. We read in the afternoon in the summertime, and we read before going to sleep. Each one of us always had multiple books piled on our bedside tables. Mother loved books.

"She's really at a loss," Tom shook his head.

She wanders around a bit more now. And since she's not reading, she doesn't have much to entertain her other than the piano. She does play the piano a lot, which is good."
"What about television?"

Tom explained that she couldn't follow many of her favorite shows anymore, like "Murder She Wrote." The plots were too complex. She would ask a lot of questions when Ann and Tom watched TV with her. When she couldn't' understand what was going on, she would say that the stories were silly and stupid, and she would often get up in a huff and turn off the TV, much to their frustration if they were engaged in the plot at the time.

John was coming soon, so the three of us would have a chance to talk and look at options. We discussed the problem. This was tough. Mother and all of us got so much joy from reading that I couldn't fathom not being able to read. Or finding it too confusing.

This was just one of many of her losses.

It was John's idea to go to the video store and look for movies that we thought she knew, and would like. We did that, hopeful that we would find something. We tried one or two, and they were dismal failures, real bombs.

Finally, we happened upon *The Sound of Music*. She had taken us to the premiere in 1964 when it first came out, at a large movie theater in San Juan. It was such a long show that it had an intermission. We all loved it. At least, I remember that Mother and I did.

So, when we played the video, we were mildly hopeful. What a pleasant surprise to find that she not only loved it, she was more engaged than we'd seen her in months. So, we tried it again the next day, and she loved it again.

Once again, we found a solution by happenstance supported with trial and error. Someone had a creative idea, and we worked with it. We kept trying things. What finally worked was born in a creative moment, and tried and tested. We had found another discovery that worked alongside a number that didn't work. , but we had tried enough videos to find the one that really clicked for her.

What we didn't know then was that she would watch *The Sound of Music* almost daily (sometimes twice a day) for the remaining few years of her life.

It nourished her in a way that was magical.

When the movie started with Julie Andrews singing in the meadow, Mother would always say "Oh, look," or "Isn't that pretty." A big smile would come across her face. She would laugh and clap her hands. From that moment that Julie Andrews spun around in the high mountain meadow until the time that the Germans came to hunt down the Von Trapp family, Mama would watch, fully engaged, excited and alive. We discovered that Mama followed the story and enjoyed things up until the time that the Gestapo were hunting the Von Trapps and they escaped. That part of the movie frightened and confused her. So we always ended the movie before that section.

It's funny that I can't remember where that was now, but we had found a good stopping point that we always used.

Little did we realize the role that ***The Sound of Music*** would play in our lives when it came out in the 1960s, or even after we re-discovered it for Mother that Christmas. But, that movie would become one of her mainstays – and ours. Every afternoon for about two years, whoever was caring for her would get her situated in front of the television and put on ***The Sound of Music***.

Each time she watched, it would be new. The story, the pictures and the music gave her many happy hours during those final years. She was actively engaged, and life had meaning, though that meaning was inexplicable to us. It was important enough to see that she would smile, clap her hands and enter into a world that gave her great joy.

My brother John and I found that we had memorized all of the songs and a great deal of the dialogue when all was said and done.

*Isn't it funny, the things we discover that work? When we realized that **The Sound of Music** would be such a help to Mama, we were pleased, surprised and fascinated. As she moved inexorably into the dimness of dementia, we were humbled by the process of discovering all along the way little things that gave her joy and enlivened her. The little things that engaged her. And those that helped her, and us, to cope.*

These were the little, and very important things that made for a better day.

We learned that one should just be open to ideas and become as creative as possible.

So, try a lot of things. It was surprising to see what works. Again, each family is different, and each person is different. So what clicked for my Mother won't necessarily click for your Mother, or Father, spouse or other loved one. However, my experience does tell me that the human spirit is strong and resilient. Even with the dimness caused by dementia, there are sparks of life and light. And when one finds a way to connect with one of those sparks, magic happens for all of us.

I strongly recommend the movie, "The Notebook," with James Garner and Gena Rowlands. It's the story of a couple who fell in love decades ago during and after World War II. The wife is now struggling with Alzheimer's, and her husband is caring for her. She goes in and out of dementia. Over time, her husband has learned how to walk with her through the ups and downs of her journey. He reads stories about their earlier life, which give her a great deal of satisfaction and joy, and which occasionally serve to spark her recollections, and her ability to reconnect with her husband and her life.

Chapter 20: Friskies and Milk for Breakfast

Mother had been living in her new house near Tom and Ann for over a year. After her plateau, she was now beginning to lose her ability to manage many other aspects of her life. For years, she had depended upon children, caregivers and friends for help with rides, grocery shopping, going to church and doctors' appointments.

Early on, before moving her to Louisville, she had needed help with many aspects of her life, especially with maintaining the house, paying bills and handling her affairs. However, after moving her to Louisville, she needed to rely on family and caregivers for much more, including cooking and eating her main meals, getting up in the morning and getting to bed at night.

Although she could sometimes dress herself, she often needed help with dressing as well. We found that when she tried to dress herself, she usually chose the clothes we had bought that were easy to put on, with no buttons or difficult openings.

She no longer read, although she continued to keep her *Daily Word* on the nightstand by her bed. It was an old issue, and that same monthly reflection stayed by her bedside for a long time. Someone had cancelled her subscription. For a person for whom reading had been a great love, it was sad to see her no longer able to engage in one of her favorite pastimes. More than a pastime, a life-giving activity.

It was difficult to see and acknowledge the decline, probably harder for us, because she didn't seem to be that aware of the loss. Thank goodness for that. She would have been horrified.

During her first years with Alzheimer's, when she left little "sticky notes" everywhere, she was constantly frustrated when she couldn't remember things and often irate when we would correct her. However, by now, she had mellowed into some sort of gentle mental fog.

She was starting to sit for long periods with the television on, staring off into space. She could still play the piano. She knew that we were important to her, loved ones with some connection she didn't understand, but accepted.

Whereas her social skills helped her a great deal in the beginning to cover up her forgetfulness, they were now weak and tawdry props. Her smile became forced and her eyes glassy. She now almost always had that dreaded "Alzheimer's look." And whereas Mama always walked with a purposeful stride, her gait was now much more of a shuffle.

On one of my visits to Louisville to provide some respite care to Tom and Ann, I had just finished breakfast when I was surprised to find Mother coming into the kitchen. Although she was an early riser for most of my life, she took to sleeping in during her final years.

I fixed her some oatmeal and we visited for a while. Focusing perhaps too much on tasks I was trying to accomplish, I got her settled in the den watching *The Sound of Music* and began my projects.

About mid-morning, my sister-in-law Ann came into the kitchen. She and I checked on Mother, who was still engrossed in Julie Andrews, the story and song. We were so lucky to have happened upon that movie to keep her occupied. We would discover soon what a joy and a mainstay for her later on when little could grasp her attention or occupy her mind.

Ann was understandably concerned about Mother's decline. Tom came by almost every day and helped Mama with a great deal. He handled the house, helped her with meals, and he would sit with her and keep her company while he graded papers. Later on, he would often spend the night.

But it was Ann who spent hours with Mother day in and day out. And I could tell she was exhausted. However, Ann never lost her sense of humor. One day she told me about Mama's very recent experience with Friskies.

One morning a few weeks before, Ann had dropped by to check up on Mama, visit with her and help her with the day's activities. As I've already mentioned, Ann would spend hours each day with Mama, and we had hired a friend of Ann and Tom's, named Robbie who was Mama's first caregiver, though we never dared use that term with Mother. Between Ann, Tom and Robbie, they provided support during many of Mother's waking hours.

That particular morning, Mother was already up, dressed and sitting at the kitchen table eating breakfast as Ann came in. She was in a good mood and offered to fix Ann some cereal and milk. Going over to the cupboard, she pulled out the box of Friskies and put it on the table. Then she got the milk from the fridge and fixed Ann a bowl. Friskies and milk.

Ann said, laughing, "I was flabbergasted. Didn't know what to do. After she fixed mine, she calmly went back to her own bowl and finished it up. I thought for a minute I'd try to stop her. But, well.

She'd already started eating it before I got there. And, I realized that stopping her might just upset her and make things worse. "

We laughed so hard we almost cried. And, if we hadn't been laughing, we might have cried.

But Ann was right. She wanted to protect Mother's dignity, and upset her as little as possible. And she wanted to avoid eating Friskies herself. So she dillied and dallied, as we say in the South, and somehow managed to finesse the issue, dump the contents in the disposal and move Mother's attention to something else.

When the decline becomes clear, we learn to manage the best we can, and prioritize things. Looking good in a matched outfit is not important if it requires difficulty dressing, or a fight. If your loved one puts on plaids and stripes with a shirt that has stains from yesterday's lunch, if they can put it on by themselves, that's a little victory, and the rest doesn't matter.

You will find that the process of caregiving, and walking with someone in their journey with dementia strips away many of life's "shoulds." It strips life down to its essentials, with just the bare essence remaining. It doesn't really matter if your Mother spills her drink or drops some food on the table, or if your Father puts some of his clothes on backwards.

So what if your parent mixes up their memories and has stories of your childhood all jumbled up. Mama had juxtaposed our childhood home in San Juan onto the Wyoming mountains. At first we argued. Soon, we realized that it really didn't matter.

Spending time together and finding ways to enjoy one another becomes much more important.

The decline was clear, and we did the best we could to manage the loss, the grief and the anger. "The 36-Hour Day" by Nancy Mace and Peter Rabins and Robert Butler's "How to Care for Aging Parents," are two of my most strongly recommended resources then. I recently learned from a friend who knew him well that Rabins himself has now contracted Alzheimer's.

It and other resources help us to have a better intellectual understanding of the disease and its progression. These resources provide a framework. It is much harder to have an emotional understanding of Alzheimer's. However, sharing with family, friends and a support group help with the emotional understanding, and with acceptance.

Another resource that can be very helpful if this fits your own spiritual and religious values is the practice of Buddhist (Vipassana) mindfulness. One can practice mindfulness while being a good Christian, Jew, or Muslim. Mindfulness teaches us that life is impermanent. And if we live in the now, we can live meaningfully, joyfully and without a great deal of pain. It's worrying about the past and catastrophizing about the future that create pain. Of course, it's easier said than done.

Each day provides its own new reckonings.

Anne Hays Egan

Chapter 21: Health Problems, Hospital and Rehab

During what was to become Mother's last few months in Louisville, she became quite ill. She was increasingly frail and unable to communicate. She got a cold which became serious. Tom and Ann were watching her carefully, and had increased their already significant level of caregiving.

By this time, they were providing Mama with almost 24/7 care. Robbie came most weekdays for a half-day or more. Ann spent much of every day with Mama. And Tom came over in the evening to fix dinner and spend the night.

As is so often the case with the elderly, a small illness or ailment can balloon into a serious malady almost overnight. This can occur because they are not aware of what's happening, or they have a hard time communicating about the issue. Also, their bodies are so much frailer that what is a health nuisance to a younger person becomes life threatening. That was the case with Mother.

Within a short amount of time, she became very ill. Tom and Ann took her to see her doctor, and he recommended immediate hospitalization. She had pneumonia and septicemia. She was so ill that I was looking at airline flights and planning a trip.

Then, within an equally short amount of time, the hospital had been able to stabilize her. They put her on a respirator with heavy doses of medication including IV antibiotics. Within a day, she was improving.

But being in a hospital with the noise and tubes was very frightening for her. Tom and Ann managed to spend a lot of time there, providing her with the comfort that comes from having a loved one nearby. I didn't learn until almost a decade later when I was writing this book that Mother had actually been more than a handful for the hospital staff and Ann during the five days in May of 2000 when she was in the hospital.

Mother was probably terrified about being in a strange place, hooked up to tubes and monitoring equipment. Afraid and unable to understand what was happening, she tried to pull off her cardiac monitoring equipment multiple times a day. She tried to pull out her IV. And, she did succeed in pulling out her catheter.

The physician and nursing staff talked with Ann and Tom, and said that they would have to restrain Mother unless someone was with her around the clock to ensure that she did not continue to interfere with her own treatment.

Tom was adamant that he didn't want Mother to have restraints. But he was in the middle of final exams, and could not be there more than a few hours from time to time. So Ann, ever the stalwart resource, stayed with Mother for those five days. She had some respite when her own Mother would come to look after things to give Ann a break.

The five days felt like forever to Mama, to Ann, and I'm sure to the staff at the hospital. Finally, after five days, Mother was stabilized. And Ann was exhausted.

It was clear that Mother would recover. However, she was so frail that it was not safe for her to return home. In just a week or so, she had gone from being able to walk on her own and handle many tasks with assistance to being unable to walk, or go to the bathroom or feed herself. She needed intensive rehabilitation and was transferred to a nursing home that was also a rehab center.

154

Mama was transferred to a very nice private pay facility in Louisville where she tried the patience of even the best of the nursing home staff. From the first day, Mother asked the staff repeatedly when she would be able to go home. She complained. She demanded. She pontificated. And she got better.

Once Mother was better and able to get around a bit, the nursing home staff tried to get her to play the piano they had in the day room. Mother's response was: "How can you expect me to perform with such inadequate equipment?" This comment from someone with mid-stage Alzheimer's! She was a piece of work.

After a number of weeks at the nursing home, Mama was discharged back home. A few months later Ann decided that it might be useful to investigate nursing home care options, in case this was needed for Mother. We knew that she had now reached another level that required even more intensive care and monitoring.

Ann called a number of facilities including that nursing home to see what options might be available. She indicated that they had cared for Mother in the recent past.

The staff responded: "There is no availability now, nor do we see any openings for the foreseeable future."

Ann felt like they really did not want to have her come back.

A parent's final years are often littered with health scares. These make us think:
"This is it. This time, they won't recover." It isn't true with everyone. But many of our frail and elderly parents have a series

of health challenges during their final years. These scares were an emotional roller coaster for us, and are for most families.

In today's world of managed health care, one needs to be very well informed about options, resources, and have a health care advocate. In most cases, one of more of the adult children will serve as the parent's health care advocate.

As an advocate you must research the different types of health care facilities that exist where your parent lives. Today, there are excellent resources online that provide ratings of doctors and hospitals. In addition, the Joint Commission provides accreditation information. Find out which hospital has the best recovery rates, the best treatment outcomes, and the lowest in-hospital infection rates. Check to see which doctors have the best ratings by patients and accreditation agencies, and which surgeons have the best surgical outcomes. All of this information is now available online. Check the resources section at the end of the book.

Discuss these issues with friends and colleagues, other family members, and people in a support group if you're part of one. It's amazing what you learn from others' experiences.

We had already developed a Health Care Power of Attorney for Mother, along with a set of Advanced Directives. So we as children were equipped with needed resources to act on her behalf. This was important, as her children were able to direct her care and act as her advocates with the hospital staff. We were able to demand that certain standards of care be met, and were able to talk with staff to come to an agreement about Mother's care to avoid using restraints. If Mother's pneumonia had worsened and if she had become critically ill as she did a few years later, these documents would have enabled us to direct both her care and instruct the medical staff about what should not be done.

Talk with your parents about their health care wishes. If possible, do this while they are still active. I have a Health Care Power of Attorney and Advanced Health Care Directives. These instruct my health care team to not engage in extraordinary measures to keep me alive just to put time in on the ventilator and add to the hospital's billing activity. Remember that the vast majority of health care expenditures occur during the final months of someone's life. I don't want to hang around to keep some bookkeeper busy.

Do some research about the Health Care Power of Attorney and Advance Directives. If your parents haven't developed these yet, talk with them about creating them and providing you with copies. Ensure that you have them in place for yourself as well. Websites provide excellent information and templates. You can either use an attorney, a self-directed option, or talk with someone who works in a local nonprofit serving older adults to see what they would recommend.

Anne Hays Egan

Chapter 22: TSA Mishaps Mess Up Travel

We were once again moving Mama.

Mother was now much more frail and forgetful. Physically, she was weak after her bout in the hospital with septicemia and the month of rehab in the nursing home. She had moved back home, but she was more forgetful, and increasingly in a mental fog.

Even with this decline, there were times when she could be her old sharp self. She continued to play the piano, and to correct me when I played something that she knew poorly; and she knew almost all of my limited repertoire.

It was time to develop a new strategy that involved a lot more care. This time, the decisions were easier, partly because we had been through this before, and partly because Mother was more compliant. It was a mixed blessing, this new level of compliance.

As a group, we talked and decided that we could move Mama out to Wyoming to live with John. We had found a place in Wyoming just a few years before and had put some of the money from the sale of Mother's Winston-Salem house into the place in Wyoming, knowing that it would be a good investment regardless of what happened.

In Louisville, Ann and Tom got Mother ready to move by talking with her about her upcoming trip to the mountains, which she loved. They got her packed and ready for another adventure. John flew into Louisville to pick her up and escort her out to Wyoming.

For those people who live on the East or West coasts, it is often shocking to discover that you must spend a full day to travel from a city like Louisville to a small town nestled in the Bighorn Mountains of Wyoming. Although our planning for this move was much easier in comparison with the one two years before, we were worried about how well Mother would be able to weather this long journey.

She had been in the hospital and the nursing home just a few months before. We knew it would be exhausting for her and for John. So Tom, Ann and John tried to be psychologically ready as well as physically prepared.

The trip started out well enough; with a morning flight out of Louisville that was not too early for Mama to get ready and out, but no so late as to put them in Casper at midnight. There were two layovers, one in Atlanta and a second in Denver. It was grueling even during the days of unencumbered flight. With TSA body scans, pat-downs and questions, it was difficult at best.

In this case, it turned into an absolute nightmare.

John was able to keep Mother occupied during the early flight and the Atlanta layover was fun with lunch and talk about Atlanta. Mother still had a good recollection of the distant past, and enjoyed stories about Atlanta, which was the big nearby city when she was growing up. Like so many Southerners, we loved Atlanta as it represented both the Old South, and the new prosperity, what with Co-Cola headquartered on Peachtree Street, Delta headquartered there, and one of the largest interstate systems in the U.S.

The flight from Atlanta to Denver was long and tiring. Mama had napped lightly, but she hadn't really slept. So, by the time she and John arrived at the Denver airport, she was tired, hungry and cranky.

As airports go, Denver can often be as difficult to navigate as
Atlanta. It is large, and it takes a while to get from one gate to
another. Mother resisted using a wheelchair on principle, and the
walks were difficult for her, even with the pedways, or mechanized
"people movers." In fact, John often avoided them because Mama
became frightened by the prospect of hopping on and off of a
moving belt. Whenever possible, they hopped on the little trams
that took people from gate to gate, as that mode of transport was
not nearly as repugnant to her as a wheelchair.

In Denver, they had to change carriers to Casper, and John was
forced to go through the TSA search once again. This time, he was
selected for a full body scan by TSA. Even though he explained to
them that he was traveling with his frail and mentally impaired
elderly Mother, they did not appear to be either sympathetic, or
even interested. He was one of their chosen, and that was that.

John tried to get the TSA staff to allow him to get Mama and bring
her along where she would be nearby, and watched by a TSA
staffer. Mama wasn't that far away at that point, certainly within
shouting distance. But they refused that request.

They whisked John away, and he felt like he was being treated
almost like a criminal, while Mother sat nearby, unaware that her
lifeline had been temporarily severed. They subjected John to a
demeaning search, and by this point, were ignoring his pleas to
watch his Mother for him while he was being detained.

Impaired as she was, Mama soon noticed that John was not there.
A few minutes later, a TSA staffer came running into the private
screening area:

"Good Lord, somebody do something. There's a crazy old lady out there screaming at the top of her lungs for Johnny. She's running up and down the aisle and nobody can calm her."

John heard that, and was furious. We children learned a great deal from Mother over the years, and one of her greatest teachings was showing us (by example) how to lay into people who are both incompetent and arrogant. We do not suffer fools lightly. The bottled up rage at the stupidity of the TSA staffers just boiled over.

"That's my Mother, you idiots. I warned you that this would happen. I asked you to bring her so she could be nearby. But, no. You wouldn't listen. Well, your stupidity has just made an elderly woman sicker, and created incalculable difficulties for the final leg of our travel. You should be ashamed of yourselves. If, in the future, you find yourselves needing to care for an elderly parent as I am doing now, I hope that you're treated better than you've treated me."

They were a bit aghast at the dressing down. A few were probably ashamed, realizing that John was right, though. TSA's decision not to deal with the customer's request was a gross oversight at best, or negligence at worst. The error had serious consequences for the travelers.

Fortunately, there was someone in a supervisory position who had a little compassion, and a little common sense. John was allowed to quickly get dressed, go round up Mother, and try to calm her down before they had to make the connecting flight.

He was angry, and Mother was terrified. Both were exhausted. She chattered meaninglessly for the rest of the evening, totally disoriented and dismayed. She had been abused, and so had John.

When you're caring for an elderly parent who is severely impaired, bureaucrats can be the bane of your existence. Bureaucrats acting badly can be disruptive, harmful, or even dangerous.

How can you cope with these types of situations?

Whether it's the TSA, or a local government official, or a staffer in a health care facility, we find that many are well trained professionals who do a good job, who have pride in their performance, and who care about those they serve.

I believe that the majority try hard and do well most days. However, there are the minority who are the officious, ignorant and arrogant staffers who can make your life a living hell, as those staffers did with Mother and John.

Your strategy really depends upon the situation. In some cases, it is possible to analyze the organization and meet with staff who are "the good ones," or to demand to see a manager. Sometimes, it is possible to demand better service, or demand a change.

When possible, having two or more people meeting with the staffer will help. And if you have a well informed advocate, most staff will take pains to do a good job because they realize that their errors won't be tolerated very well. It's wonderful to have an advocate.

However, there will be those times when all of the best planning doesn't provide safety or protection. There are times when it is not practical or affordable to have an advocate with you, as was true on this plane trip. And in those times, if it all goes to pieces, then you just do the best you can.

Prepare as best you can. Use an advocate where possible.

When the bad stuff happens (and it will), draw upon your best coping strategies. For some it is withdrawal and silence. For others, it's a demand.

We all do the best we can.

Chapter 23: Afternoon Drives in the Bighorns

Buffalo is a small town of about 4,000 people nestled at the foot of the Bighorn Mountains, near Sheridan in northeast Wyoming. Once John got Mama to the house in Buffalo, he looked for things he could do to help her settle in. One of his first ideas became a mainstay for him and for Mama. He took her out for afternoon drives in the Bighorns.

The scenery around Buffalo is stunning: large craggy peaks, high mountain meadows full of flowers in the summer, cows and cattle drives, deer, antelope, and a cobalt blue sky with a limitless horizon. So he took some time in the afternoons to explore the region where the deer and the antelope really do play, along with a lot of other wildlife.

They drove through the countryside every day, usually in the afternoon. He would drive up into the nearby mountains where they would visit South Fork – not the one in Texas, but rather a horse ranch. They would drive to Ucross, a foundation and artists' colony. They would drive over to Sheridan or up into the heavily wooded tiny town of Story, with a population of a few hundred people and hundreds of thousands of beautiful pine trees.

Her eyesight and her sense of perspective were changing, and she did not realize that the mountains were many thousands of feet high and miles away. In fact, the peaks and passes are above 10,000 feet. She thought they were hills close by. I'm not sure if one's ability to see or process three dimensional viewing is lost with Alzheimer's. But her perspective had flattened along with her affect and her face.

She did enjoy the drives. John varied them, and pointed out scenic markers, wildlife and cattle. Going back to old activities Mama played on long car trips with us as children, John had her count the cattle, or look for red cars. He would point out simple things like ranch houses. There was an ugly pile of used cars way out in the countryside, and, true to form, Mother always made a negative comment about it, and John used this as a way to develop conversation. He also would call out when they crossed a cattle guard in the road:

"Get ready for bumpety bump," he would say. And then: "Here's bumpety bump." "Bumpety bump," she would respond.

It was so very basic that it almost seems silly sharing it. However, it engaged her. She was involved in conversation, and interacting with John and the environment. It made her happy.

As part of my work developing the book, I have thought about many of the experiences we had caring for Mama. I've reflected upon our decisions and their impact on all of us. And, I've considered the strange way that answers came to us.

The drives, and the "bumpety bump" conversations were examples of a strategy we employed intuitively. We talked about whatever seemed to come up, and tailored our conversations to wherever she happened to be at the moment.

Over time, we were guided by the following very basic principles. They made sense and worked for us. Perhaps some will work for you.

1. *Keep Mama safe, clean, and dressed;*
2. *Give her lots of small high-calorie and high-nutrition food and milkshakes;*
3. *Provide a routine that offers reassurance;*
4. *Hire compassionate and competent caregivers;*
5. *Develop ways to engage and occupy her (**The Sound of Music**, drives in the country, piano, and helping to prepare meals or set the table);*
6. *Engage in whatever conversation works;*
7. *Forget about reality-based discussions and stay with stories;*
8. *Look for simple ways to enjoy time with Mama;*
9. *Take care of ourselves.*

Chapter 24: Nutritional Challenges: Getting Her to Eat

Like so many people who are elderly, frail and suffer from Alzheimer's, Mama lost her appetite. She didn't have much of one to begin with, so this was a serious problem. Thin and svelte for most of her life, except during menopause, she was in the low three figures, as we were saying then. And, too often, she had dipped into the high two figures. Mama was just under 5'7" and a two figure weight represented a serious health hazard.

Again, Mama's care for her own Mother gave us guidance with the issue. During her mid and late nineties, Gram had pretty much lost her interest in eating. They say that we lose some of our sense of taste as we become elderly. And eating becomes a bit of a chore.

Mama had tried many different strategies to get Gram to eat. Like us, she experimented with many options, and her most successful was a high-protein, high-calorie milk shake. John used the recipe Mama developed for Gram as his base. Mama's own milkshake included milk, chocolate ice cream (new), chocolate syrup, blackstrap molasses, protein powder (new) and part of a banana. John also added a vitamin mix. Blended in the right proportion, it tasted good and was probably close to 500 calories.

The milkshakes worked, and quickly became a mainstay for Mama. By feeding her a milkshake once or twice a day, he was able to help her from losing any more weight. And, from time to time, she actually gained a little weight.

But her weight always remained low, and it was a challenge.

Most of us become pickier with our food as we age. Our appetites are reduced, and we eat smaller portions. That's not always the case, but is often the case with women, and it was true for both Gram and Mother.

Gram loved chocolate all of her life, and one way to stack up the calories was to give her candy, ice cream or cookies. Mama's sweet tooth wasn't as well developed as Gram's, but she did like ice cream and cookies, so those became her food staples along with the milkshakes.

Every once in a while, some well-meaning but impractical health professional would ask about her nutrition and recommend things like more green leafy veggies. We were somewhere entirely different on Maslow's Hierarchy of Needs. We were simply trying to get her to eat enough calories to keep her going, with as much nutrition, vitamins and protein as we could get into her. We still served her lunch and dinner, but she picked at her food, and got little nutrition from the traditional meals. So we were simply not able to deal with higher order issues like green leafy veggies. We tried to give her good tasting, high protein and high calorie shakes. They worked, and that's what was important to us.

Even though the shakes represented her main meals, John continued to have breakfast, lunch, and dinner at the dining room table. This was another of the important rituals that could help ground Mama and reassure her.

Sometimes Mother surprised us, and would come to the table with an appetite. Those times became less frequent with the progression of her dementia, and her increasing frailty. And, it was always a joyful occasion when she was hungry, and interested in food.

In addition to losing our appetites as we age, we often become more isolated, and preparing nutritious meals becomes a hassle. As we become more elderly and frail, nutrition often poses a challenge.

My cousin Jenny mentioned that she and Carolyn had a similar challenge with their Mother Tula. Her sense of taste diminished, and food no longer tasted very good. Jenny also experimented with different options, choosing those foods that her Mother liked best.

Although it is ideal for one to eat nutritious, healthy meals, as people age, it becomes more important to ensure that people are eating – period. And that they receive needed vitamins, other nutrients, protein and calories. I'm not a nutritionist, and am way out of my depth here. However, many who have been involved with caregiving have shared similar experiences and a similar decision making process.

There are some wonderful local resources to help both you and your parents as you look at nutrition. Senior Centers are funded by the federal government to provide nutritious mid-day meals. Governmental leaders at federal and state levels realize that older adults often do not eat well. So these meals provide excellent mid-day nutrition for a small donation. Many Senior Centers or the local Meals on Wheels also provide home delivered meals.

Senior Centers and local college and university continuing education departments and other nonprofits offer presentations and workshops on nutrition, nutrition and aging, and other related topics.

Anne Hays Egan

Chapter 25: Personal Care, Dr. Whorton's RX and Skin Treatments

A number of times Mother's caregivers had tried to get her to wear adult diapers. She needed the protection, but she fought the efforts with such force that they always backed down. After she moved to Wyoming, her incontinence started to become a problem and she was damaging her favorite chair and parts of the rug.

Clean-up was a poor choice, but she still fought efforts to get her into diapers. What a mess it was. Literally.

Soon after she arrived in Wyoming, I was up visiting and witnessed the ongoing fights. When we were growing up, she and we used to call them "knock down drag out fights." Only, this time, our roles had reversed. The arguments were terrible. Something had to be done.

Finally, John and I had an idea. Again, it was just one of those wild ideas that "popped into our heads." By this time, we had learned to pay attention to those intuitive flashes, because they usually provided a helpful solution.

This time, we found ourselves talking about her Father, Dr. Whorton. She worshipped him because, as I mentioned earlier, he had performed a lifesaving appendectomy on her burst appendix when she was a child. He was a well-known Birmingham doctor prone to rages and drink, but he was a force in her young life – both a positive and negative one.

And we discovered that his force still held sway for Mama.

I found myself telling another tale:

"Mama," I said. You know that your Father, Dr. Whorton wants you to wear these special pants for your back."

"For my back?" she asked.

"Yes, Mama. He checked you out, and you need some more back support."

She gave me one of her looks, but I persevered, already deep into this wild tale.

"Mama, they will really help you. They give you support for your lower back."

I held them up to myself, pointing to the back of them, and my back.

"Please, Lord. Let this one fly," I thought.

"Oh, all right. If he said so."

"He did, Mama. He did," I said.

And so Mama wore her adult diapers every day from then until the day she died, without complaint, and without any further arguments.

John was especially relieved

Mama was bathing less. By this point, she was in the later stages of Alzheimer's and she really didn't notice much of anything, including bathing and dressing. She had help each morning getting dressed. Meals were now an interactive event with someone helping her to eat or drink. And, she was helped each evening to go to bed.

John and we became concerned about her personal hygiene, bathing and brushing her teeth. We didn't do very well with the tooth brushing, but we did find a way to get her to let someone give her a bath.

When we talked about having someone help her bathe, she would argue with us, stonewall us, deride us, or stomp out. Her defense mechanisms were well honed, and she could use them until a few months before her death.

Like many women of her generation, she was extremely modest and didn't like the idea of being undressed by a caregiver. And, she was probably afraid of water by that time.

As we talked with one of her caregivers, I was hit by another intuitive flash, and found myself telling her another story.

"Mama," I said. "Jolene is here to give you a skin treatment." Skin treatment, I asked myself. Where in the world did that come from?

"A skin treatment?" She echoed a bit incredulously.
"Yes, they're very special, and so good for you."

So I spun the tale. I don't remember now if I invoked the long dead ghost of her Father Dr. Whorton or not. But whatever was said seemed to do the trick. Mama allowed Jolene to give her a bath.

We never referred to the bath by its proper name again. It was always a skin treatment. And, she never fought the bath again, but allowed Jolene to bathe her. Only Jolene.

And, that was fine with everyone else.

Some of the most difficult issues we face in caregiving include incontinence, not bathing, wandering, and problems with elimination. Mother didn't wander, which was a blessing.

If your elderly parent starts to bathe or shower less, or actively resists that well entrenched ritual, you're not alone. People with dementia will gradually lose their capacity to handle their daily tasks, including self-care. They forget how to bathe and how to dress themselves. Some can actually come to fear water.

Look at eldercare websites and talk with friends and colleagues. Develop a list of tips and strategies that would, or might be helpful in your situation. Every person is different, but there are probably ways that you can approach personal care challenges that make the solution a bit easier, rather than harder.

Often, we can benefit from talking with a professional caregiver, a staff person at a local Senior Center, or someone who has dealt with these specific issues. I believe that good caregivers have developed an amazing set of skills that help them deal successfully with all of these challenges.

Remember that these are challenging situations for everyone. You're looking for progress here. Do the best you can.

Chapter 26: Managing Sundowners – Her Mother's Summer at Columbia

Mother continued to decline during the almost two years she lived with John in Wyoming. My visits became more frequent because I now lived closer to Mama than I had before. We had excellent caregivers, and John was amazing in the way he managed.

Mama had a wonderful quality of life almost impossible to most people in such a state of advanced dementia. Almost every day, John or one of the caregivers took her out for a drive. She loved to see the birds, the mountains and the antelope. She found the wildlife fascinating and looked forward to the drives. They were moments of joy for her.

She continued to play the piano. At this point, she didn't have the skill she'd had in earlier years, but she could still play quite a few tunes, especially "Tea for Two" and other World War II-era songs. With John's assistance, she was asked once or twice to go to the Senior Center to play. She reluctantly agreed, often saying: "Well, I'll go, but I won't stay. I don't have anything in common with those old folks." She went. She played. And she never stayed for lunch. Oh, well. It was a good idea.

Every day near dusk, which was 4 pm in the winter in Wyoming, she would begin to become agitated. She would usually be finished with *The Sound of Music* by mid to late afternoon. And, if she didn't watch it twice, she would look out the window.

We'd have to watch her because she would also often open the door, heating the outdoors and causing the inside temperature to plummet. She would wander back and forth between the living room, dining room and kitchen. And as the sky became darker, she would usually say: "It's getting late. I have to get back home to Mama."

Her Mama and our "Gram" was born in 1882 and she had died in 1982, almost twenty years before Mama's Wyoming days. In fact, Mother and Dad had taken care of Gram at home during her last years. Mother was the baby of the family and she and Gram were extremely close. And she gave Gram nothing but the best, most tender loving care possible.

Mother would keep talking about needing to go, and we would try to distract her or soothe her. But she experienced our efforts as keeping her from getting back to her Mother. I remember many times trying to get her to focus on something else, like playing the piano. It didn't work. She could not be distracted.

As the sky would darken, she would become increasingly agitated, begging us to help her get on the road and back home to Birmingham and her Mother. It was painful and exhausting. We tried so many things. Nothing seemed to work.

All three of us would talk from time to time about the problem with Sundowner's Syndrome. Most people with Alzheimer's are affected with this syndrome. As the sun begins to set, they become agitated and are often fearful of the darkening world. Turning up the lights helped somewhat, but only as a temporary placating device.

Finally, late one afternoon during one of my visits, she began the litany again about needing to leave, to go home to her Mother. I'm not sure where I got the idea, but I said "Mama, don't you remember? Gram isn't home right now. She got an award to study

art at Columbia in New York. She's in New York at the art institute."
Snap.

"She is?" She said. "Oh, all right." Somehow I had found the answer that calmed her. Over the rest of that evening and the remainder of my visit, when Mother expressed concerns about needing to go back home to her Mama, I would explain that she was up in New York at Columbia studying art.

It worked. It really worked.

As I've mentioned, back in the late 1920s or early 1930s, Gram had been an award-winning Southern artist, well known for her commissioned portraits of Jefferson Davis and House Speaker Bankhead (Father of the famous Tallulah Bankhead). And Gram did go to Columbia one summer in the 1920s to study art. It was a highlight for her and for Mama, and they talked about it with a great deal of fondness. I believe Mother may have even gone up to visit her in New York that summer, as there are quite a few pictures of them "doing the town," hats and all.

Like so many of the solutions we found for Mama's care, this one came as an intuitive brainstorm, "out of the blue." These solutions were not rationally deduced at all. Rather, a creative idea would just come to us and we would try it out.

That happened with my response to her when she said to me "You look so familiar," when we were at my Cousin Jenny's house before Tula's memorial service. It was that same intuitive "hit" with *The Sound of Music*. It was that creative brainstorming that convinced us we could move Mama and make it all a story, an adventure.

For much of the remaining year or two of her life, Mother would talk about needing to get back to Birmingham to take care of her Mother. And, we would remind her that Gram was at Columbia studying art. She would nod, remembering that fact. And she would be comforted.

Chapter 27: Taking Time and Living in the Now

Caring for Mama during her final years with Alzheimer's taught me the importance of living in the now. Time was a shape-shifting enemy for all of us, and we never knew what a new day would bring. Over the years, we changed our expectations.

It was no longer important to have reality-based conversations. We just talked about whatever interested her in the moment. Sometimes our conversations would go something like this:

"Oh, Mama. See the bird?"
"Where?"
"Over there. In the tree"
"Pretty. I like the birds."
"Hear the birds. They are singing."
"Yes, singing birds."

"Look, there goes a car."
"Isn't that a big car?"
"That car's too big."
"I know, I wouldn't want to drive a car that big."
"I like our car."

And we would talk that way about almost everything during the last nine months or so of her life. It kept her connected. And it kept both of us grounded.

By this time, Mother had lost a good bit of her vocabulary. Thank goodness, she had a very large one to begin with. Building your vocabulary has a new level of importance for me now. She had a lot to start with, and she was able to cope a lot longer than most.

We would watch ***The Sound of Music*** together. Once or twice a day.

We would go for rides.

I would play the piano. And she would play the piano. Although her repertoire diminished substantially, she could still play a few pieces until a few months before she died.

We would listen to music, and John would often play the piano for us. He composed, and it was always a treat to hear him play something new he had just finished.

Her favorite foods became a much bigger deal, and we would "ooh" and "aah" over candy, cookies and ice cream.

We would read selections from some of her favorite authors, focusing on old, well-loved and well known writings. Mama had been an English major and loved Shakespeare. We would read from some of the bard's best known dialogues. She enjoyed a popular news anchor who wrote a book about traveling through the U.S., and John read sections of that book to her for many months. We read the 23rd Psalm. We said the Lord's Pray at night.

Sometimes, we would just sit.

I believe that spending time with a loved one doing simple things is a blessing, and it was one of the gifts of Mother's Alzheimer's. We were forced to focus on the basics, the simplest things.

It was helpful to just sit with her.

We live in a society in the U.S. that values talk and action. However, we have a growing trend focused on spirituality, mindfulness and living in the present. It can be very helpful to both us and to our loved one with Alzheimer's to just sit together. You might read, or work on a report, or sit and watch the scenery.

Or just sit.

Being present with someone during the last part of their life provides a gift to both.

Anne Hays Egan

Chapter 28: Thanksgiving, My Last Visit with Mama

My last, and one of my nicest visits with Mama, was Thanksgiving of 2002. By this time, she was talking very little. She had lost some more weight and was quite frail.

I had decided that I would take some extra time and spend close to a week visiting. I had been quite a workaholic during my younger and middle adult years, and I was in a period where I had made some progress in developing a more balanced life. I am so glad I took that extra time.

What stands out for me as I remember that visit was how calm and peaceful we both were. It was just a nice time all around. It was pleasant and easy. And that, in our family, is a major accomplishment.

She and I spent a lot of time together, just sitting and talking about little things. We watched *The Sound of Music* together.

We went on a lot of rides through the Wyoming countryside, counting cattle, and deer and antelope.

And, we just sat. Companionably, often in silence or with limited conversation.

It was a pleasant and unhurried time.

I realized that she was very frail, and would probably not last much longer. I just didn't realize that it would happen so quickly.

By this time, Mama was extremely frail. In spite of the many supercharged high calorie-high protein shakes we made for her, she consumed little, and her weight had dropped to just over 90 pounds.

Her vocabulary had shrunk even more than her body. The once articulate and well-read master of the right phrase could only utter a few comments. Her brain was full of the deadly plaque, slowly choking it off through its maddening proliferation, like the Alabama kudzu.

When people talk about the impact of Alzheimer's, they usually mention two things:

- **<u>The disease robs people of their very essence</u>. It takes their brains, and their ability to think, communicate and act.**

- **Even when they are severely impaired, <u>a spark remains and we can still connect in some way.</u>**

Both are true.

Chapter 29: Her Last Day - Debussy, Our Good-byes and the 23rd Psalm

Like most caregivers, I was juggling too much, overly stressed, and not taking enough time for rest. Pushing myself to finish work deadlines before returning to Wyoming, I was driving back to Santa Fe from a long day of meetings out of town when stress caught up with me. Driving tired and distracted, I had a car accident that was serious enough to total my car.

After the officer onsite took my information, I called John to let him know what happened. John responded with the strangest comments:

"I'm so glad you called," he said.
"Why?"
"Because Mother has been agitated and upset for the last half hour or so. She's been asking about you, saying 'what's wrong with Anne Hays ?' "
"What?"
"Yes, she's been very upset. She's been pacing, asking about you. Worried that something bad had happened."

As I talked with them both, I realized that Mama was more present, articulate and connected than I had seen her in a while. I reassured them that I was all right, but shaken.

The police officer on the scene was wonderful, and he offered to take me to a hotel after we finished the paperwork.

Later, both John and I agreed that the incident was really strange. I've believed for a long time that the veil between this world and the next can often be quite thin. I've also believed that there are many different ways of knowing. Somehow, both seemed to have been present in that situation. I can't figure it out, and don't try. There had been an incredibly powerful connection which has meant a great deal to me in the years since.

The next week, and the last week before my return to Wyoming, my "To Do" List had grown to include finding a new car. During the beginning of the second week of December, John and I talked daily and sometimes a few times a day. Mother had caught a cold and was not feeling well, and we were both worried.

When I talked with Mother on the phone, she sounded chipper but tired and frail. I had planned to drive back up to Wyoming in mid-December, after winding up some meetings scheduled on a new project. John felt that Mother might be slipping, but neither of us thought she would decline as quickly as she did.

A few days before I was scheduled to go to Wyoming, John and I had a long talk about Mother's condition. He reported that she had been feeling sicker, that caregivers were spending additional time with her, and the Visiting Nurse Service nurse was coming more often. I offered to come up earlier and reschedule the meetings, but after further discussion we both felt that it would be fine for me to drive up on the 17th.

Sometime earlier in the day the 17th, John told me that Mother's breathing had become labored, and that he and Dottie from VNS had asked her if she wanted to go to the hospital. She said "no." Dottie had discussed the pros and cons of putting Mother on oxygen, as her blood oxygen levels were beginning to decline.

John talked with Tom and me about this. We all agreed that the oxygen would simply prolong the inevitable, and that Mother would probably be frightened of the tubes. It was one of the toughest decisions we ever made. We also knew that it was exactly the decision Mother would have made for herself. I gained a newfound appreciation of Mother's stand-off with the young doctor when Gram was dying.

We did decide to enroll Mother in hospice care, which turned out to last for little over a day. The caregivers and VNS nurse who had been with her for so long were the real anchors for her and for us.

I worked to wrap up, and headed north straight from my meetings in Taos, through the mountains. By the time I was entering Colorado, a snowstorm had started. And by the time I reached Monument South of Denver, the slopes had iced and traffic was at a near standstill.

However, the Colorado crews were finally able to clear the roads. Driving past Denver, I realized that I would probably be able to make Buffalo that night, just very late. During the late afternoon and evening, I had been talking with John and Mother.

When I stopped for gas in Cheyenne, I called again and had what was to be my last conversation with Mama. I reassured her once again that I was on my way, would be there soon and that I loved her. She told me she loved me, too.

I drove as fast as I could, but missed her last moments by just a few hours. Initially, I was devastated. But as I lived with the loss, I realized that we had said good-bye in a sense at Thanksgiving, with that peace-filled, joyful few days of being together. John allowed her to slip away naturally, without any extraordinary measures, as she wanted.

John is one of those rare people with a stratospherically high IQ and a limitlessly compassionate heart. His care for Mother during her last few days was a testament to both.

Knowing her wishes, he gathered the caregiving resources to surround her in the ways she wanted. When Mama was no longer able to get out of bed, a day or so before her death, he had the piano moved into her room so that she could hear him playing.

Throughout the last day, he would play Mozart, Bach, Ravel and Debussy. He made sure that she was supported in her journey by her familiar favorites like Bach's **Sheep May Safely Graze**, and Debussy's **Girl with The Flaxen Hair** as well as some of her most loved hymns. He read the **23rd Psalm**.

About a half hour after my call to them from Cheyenne, Mother slipped out of consciousness. Her breathing slowed and became more shallow. John later told me that Betsy Blue Eyes, one of her cats, came to lie beside her head as she was slipping away.

Tom and Ann came out to join us a day or two later, and the four of us made funeral plans, which were rather complex and included a service in Wyoming, a burial in the family plot in Birmingham, and a memorial in Winston-Salem where Mother and Dad had lived for 30 years.

For quite some time, we second guessed our decisions. Should she have gone to the hospital? Was it appropriate to defer the oxygen? Should I have cancelled my meetings and left earlier?

Over time, we realized that each of us did the best we could, given the conditions of the day. We worked together as a team, and made decisions jointly, which was amazing and very much unlike our often dysfunctional family dynamic. We consulted one another, and we did try to do what we thought Mother wanted, and what was best for her.

There is a great deal we learned from the experience, and we talked about this together as we managed the funeral and her affairs.

*****

Anne Hays Egan

Resources for Caregiving

The following provides a list of helpful resources for you as you look at providing care to your parent, spouse or other loved one. I have included a summary of key issues you may want to address, noting websites that I have found to be helpful, and local and state resources. These are current as of the fall of 2013, and many will be changed or updated over time. For current information, please visit my website, www.movingMama.net.

These core community resources are described based on the category or type of service. National leading resources are listed at the end of the article, with links to their websites.

Sometimes it is difficult to identify needed community resources to help with an elderly person's care. Professionals in related fields may find that caregiving resources grow and change quickly, and it can be difficult to keep up with these changes. Family members are even more confused as they try to discover and then access appropriate resources. Some of the confusion comes from not knowing what types of resources to research, and what types of payments are required, or insurance plans accepted, and whether sliding fee scale or free services are available.

A. Older Adult Services: The Big Picture

The "backbone" of community services for the elderly has been the Administration on Aging funded federal Title XX services for older adults authorized by the Older Americans Act.. The Older Americans Act, was initially passed in 1965, and reauthorized most recently in 2011. It establishes the federal Administration on Aging to oversee and fund older adult services. The law provides the policies, defines the services, and describes the funding parameters for older adults in every U.S. state and territory.

In 1973-1974, the federal Administration on Aging established Area Agencies on Aging and funding for social services for older adults through the states. In the early 1980s, the Administration on Aging was involved in nursing home reform through an omnibus reconciliation act. Later, it dealt with the growing demand for and regulation of caregivers, discrimination against the elderly and elder rights.

B. Core Administration on Aging Funded Community Resources

Core social service, nutrition, transportation and home care programs at the community level are often funded through Administration on Aging grants to the states. Many of these services are offered through a county or local city Senior Center. Senior Centers are often nonprofit agencies, however some centers are run by local government entities. In larger communities, one can find more than one Title XX funded organization.

For more information about Title XX funded services, contact the Administration on Aging's website by typing in those words, and/or contact your state's Agency on Aging.

C. Other Community Resources

There are a number of services in many local communities. The larger the community, the greater and more diverse the programs and services. The following represent some of the most frequently found local resources.

<u>Senior Centers</u> - These provide a range of services to older adults, usually age 60 and older. They are usually funded for a range of social, educational and fitness activities; lunch and nutrition services; transportation, and often some level of visiting and/or home care services. Many centers that are nonprofits receive additional funding from grants, contracts and donors which allows them to further develop and expand services beyond core services funded by the Agency on Aging.

Visiting Nurse Services (VNS) - Located in most major metropolitan areas, Visiting Nurse Services is a nonprofit home health care agency founded almost 100 years ago. It provides home health care and hospice services in many communities. Services to older adults comprise a large portion of many local VNS agencies. VNS home care services allow many older adults to remain in their homes by providing assistance to help people with basic activities of daily living (ADLs).

Meals on Wheels - Local Meals on Wheels programs provide home delivered meals to home bound people five days a week. Services to older adults represent a significant part of home delivered meals.

Local Hospice Organizations - Many communities have a freestanding local hospice nonprofit agency or a hospice program related to a local hospital or other large organization. Large metro areas may have multiple hospice programs. Hospice care is a critically needed part of the service mix, and a growing need.

Caregiving - nonprofits and businesses provide a range of caregiving services. Some of the strongest in the field have excellent quality records. Check thoroughly, as there is a large difference among local providers and with the quality of care provided.

Counseling - available in many different settings, there are therapists with expertise in family counseling as well as working with adult children of frail elderly. Look for this expertise.

Legal Issues - these often include developing financial and health care Power of Attorney or general Power of Attorney. Other issues can include developing wills and trusts, identifying affairs that need to be handled by the adult children, and, in some cases guardianship. In some communities, there are Senior Citizens' Law resources that provide pro bono and/or sliding fee scale services. Find attorneys with expertise in elder law.

Financial Issues - in addition to those mentioned above, many families find that the costs for elder care can be excessive, sometimes stripping family resources. Resources can include nonprofit sliding fee scale services, dual eligible Medicare/Medicaid coverage, and county health care funds in many states

D. National Resources, with Website Links

The following include a list of some of the most popular and helpful national resources, updated from time to time as needed.

Administration on Aging. The federal Administration on Aging (AOA) provides funding and resources to all U.S. states and territories for a range of programs for older adults. States provide funding for a number of important community based programs, to include local Senior Centers. In many communities, funding also covers some level of home care, transportation and respite care. The AOA has extensive website resources, and is recommended as a "first stop" in your research. Check your state Agency on Aging website for more information about local community resources.

Alzheimer's Association The Alzheimer's Association has been a major resource in the field of aging for decades, and provides excellent resources about the disease. It offers practical information and guidance to help caregivers to cope with the impact of Alzheimer's on families. Also provides contacts for local chapters and community resources.

AARP - American Association of Retired Persons AARP is one of the largest associations in the U.S., with a membership base in the tens of millions. They provide information, resources and referrals on many topics of concern to older adults and their families.

Benefits Check Up Benefits Check Up is a comprehensive website that provides information about benefits that may be available to you or your loved one. It's a simple way to discover what may be available for you.

Healthfinder Site hosted by the federal government's Department of Health and Human Services. Provides health information and resources.

Medicare Critically important federal government resource describing the Medicare program, types of plans and policies, and covered conditions. Also includes information about fraud and links to other helpful government publications. Website lists state and local community resources, and information about nearby local government offices that can help.

National Alliance for Caregiving (NAC) NAC is a non-profit coalition of national organizations focusing on issues of family caregiving. Alliance members include grassroots organizations, professional associations, service organizations, disease-specific organizations, a government agency, and corporations. NAC has a great deal of information on its website, including research findings, resources for caregivers, and information about state and local coalitions. It also provides updates about important legislation.

National Clearinghouse: Long Term Care Information This U.S. Department of Health and Human Services website provides information and resources to help families plan for future long-term care (LTC) needs. The site provides information about long term care, how to pay for services, resources and links to state and local community resources.

National Family Caregivers Association (NFCA) NFCA provides support, resources and advocacy to the more than 65 million Americans who care for loved ones with a chronic illness, disability or the frailties of old age. The website provides resources and information, and has a program to connect caregivers. It also provides information about advocacy and legislative issues.

*****

I hope that these resources are helpful to you. They are current as of August, 2013. Resource section names should be active hyperlinks, connecting you to the website of that resource. Please consult the Moving Mama website for updated resources, posts and other suggested reading material.

Thanks so much for purchasing this book.

Anne Hays Egan,
New Ventures Consulting
August 20, 2013

ABOUT THE AUTHOR

Anne Hays Egan is an organizational development consultant based near Santa Fe, NM. She has worked extensively with community and regional health planning, service coordination and community needs assessments. She has helped agencies to plan and fund service networks, including services to older adults.

She is also known as a researcher and writer in the field, and has published widely on topics related to community health, nonprofit organizations, public policy and nonprofits, and building effective programs and services. She was the publisher of *The Digest of Nonprofit Management*; contributing author to *Social Policy & Aging*, Carroll L. Estes, ed.; and is an EzineArticles expert author.

Anne lived in shared housing with Maggie Kuhn, the founder of the Gray Panthers, who was one of her models and mentors. She is a retired Presbyterian minister who loves to travel. She plays violin in the Santa Fe Community Orchestra and has a cat, Baby Doll who does tricks.

She provides information and resources through her websites, www.nonprofitsonline.net and www.movingmama.net.

Contact Anne at www.movingmama.net for information on scheduling her to come and speak to your group, or to work with her to use the book as a fund raiser for your agency.

Made in the USA
Lexington, KY
12 July 2017